1619, THE TIMES OF THE GENTILES & THE SEED OF JUDAH

SPECIAL EDITION

From the Line of Shem and Hebrew
West Africa until Messiah

Stephen Hanks

For more information about this title or to
order other books, contact the publisher:

Stephen Hanks
shankbibletalk@yahoo.com
Youtube.com/Portrait Pioneers of Color

ISBN: 978-1-7366786-3-3 (Paperback)

Printed in the United States of America

Cover and Interior design:
Van-garde Imagery • van-garde.com

Contents

CHAPTER 1

From Ndongo to Hampton

The Bakongo, or Kongo, a Bantu people, migrated into Central Africa at least before the 5ᵗʰ Century. These Kikongo-speaking people developed farming methods as well as a sophisticated culture and social infrastructure. The kingdom of Kongo was established by the 14ᵗʰ Century.

The Mbundu, also a Bantu people, arrived in the region of Central Africa in large numbers between the 13ᵗʰ and 16ᵗʰ Centuries. This Kimbundu-speaking tribe met the indigenous Pygmies and Khoi-San peoples and began trading and sharing their ancient knowledge of agriculture with these nomadic hunter-gatherers, who had been displaced by the Bantu peoples. The Mbundu were once vassals of the Kongo empire, who occupied their territories and became a Kongo province starting in 1370.

Unlike kings in Europe, who emerged based upon hereditary succession, the court nobles from the Kongo people selected the Kongo king on election. But the king was also required to recognize his peers and follow the religious rituals. Near the Atlantic coast, Kongo had many trading centers and distribution points. But in time a threat would line up, a foreign power, the Portuguese, who would come to expand their territories and become a rich lucrative player in the Atlantic Slave Trade.

In 1483, the Catholic Portuguese arrived in Central Africa, sailing up the Congo River trying to search for a sea route to India.

Instead, they met the Bakongo people and established relations with the kingdom, being allowed to setup a trading post at Soyo, which was within Ndongo territory. The Portuguese noticed Kongo's well-developed transport systems from the interior to their settlement port by the Atlantic coast. They also found the Kongo culture open to new ideas and willing to exchange trading goods. Kongo King Nzinga even adopted a Portuguese name, Joao I, and was open to exploring the Portuguese's religion, accepting their rites of baptism upon himself in 1491. Trade and cultural exchange between the two countries accelerated. The king sent Bakongo nobles to visit the royal court in Portugal, while Portugal sent their missionaries to Kongo, who converted to Catholicism, yet retaining their religious rituals and traditions.

At first, the exchange of trading items such as ivory, copper, and other goods between Kongo and Portugal was economically fair and well balanced. But soon, the Portuguese's desire turned towards purchasing Kongo's slave labor in order to operate their sugarcane fields. Not satisfied with Kongo's supply, the Portuguese began kidnapping Bakongo people, as well as provoking military campaigns in other nearby regions for their slave labor after 1500. Another change that resulted under Portuguese presence occurred in 1509, when a new Kongo king, Joao's son Afonso I, succeeded him. This was not by the usual elections from the nobles, but instead was handed down, in the style the Europeans did business in. Under King Afonso I, social disorder arose among the Kongo people due to the issue of exporting of slaves. King Afonso I wrote letters to the king of Portugal to protest the way in which the Portuguese were obtaining their slaves in the region. The Portuguese began approaching Kongo's other trading partners at the borders of the Kongo kingdom, and exchanged with them for slaves. One such slave-trading entity on Kongo's border was the Kingdom of Abyssinia (See Chapter 15). King Afonso could not stop the tide for the increasing demand in slaves and gave in. By 1520, 2,000 to 3,000 slaves were being exported per year. By the 1560's, it would become over 7,000 slaves per year. The Kingdom of Kongo had been trading in slaves way before the Portuguese arrived. But now they had become a major supplier for the Portuguese traders.

Ndongo, with the desire for independence from Kongo ever growing, sent an embassy to Portugal in 1518 asking for missionaries and to be recognized as an independent kingdom. Two years later, Portugal sent missionaries to Ndongo in 1520, but due to local disputes the missionaries withdrew. In 1556 the ruler, or Ngola of Ndongo, King Ndambi sent another mission to Portugal, this time seeking military assistance and an offer to be baptized by the Portuguese. However, this second mission to be recognized by Portugal failed. Portugal sent missionaries and Jesuit priests, who arrived at the mouth of the Kwanza River in 1560. But the new Ngola (ruler), Kiluanji kia Ndambi suspected them of being agents of Kongo and had them imprisoned. Ndongo led a war against Kongo and defeated them. So Ndongo was now independent, and remained in that position for several decades. Their capital became Kabasa, a large town comprising a population of 50,000.

Fifteen years later, the Portuguese set out to establish a colony in Kongo for the purpose of conquest and subjugation, as was authorized by the King of Portugal, Sebastian I. Settlers were brought in, forts were built, and by 1575 the colony of "Portuguese Angola" was formed with four hundred soldiers, and their capital at Luanda. Unable to conquer any Kongo territory, Governor Dias de Novais ended up making alliances with both Kongo and Ndongo. But by 1579, the Portuguese who had settled in Kongo advised Ndongo's king, Njinga Ndambi Kilombo kia Kasenda, that Portugal planned to take over his country. Njinga Ndambi tricked the Portuguese soldiers into an ambush, massacred them, and this triggered a Portuguese – Ndongo War. Portugal's invasion into Kongo was narrowly defeated, but the Portuguese were able to establish a second fort at Massangano. Unforeseen by Kongo, several of the Sobas, small province chieftains, switched their allegiance to Portugal, and resulted in many of the coastal provinces siding with the Portuguese colony and making an attack on Ndongo and its capital Kabasa in 1590. Ndongo was able to defeat the offensive with help from their alliance with the Matamba, a powerful neighbor State. So Ndongo won the attack, but the Portuguese retained much of the land they had gained from earlier wars. By 1599, Portugal and Ndongo formalized their border.

The two powers held peace, but only for a time. Between 1615 – 1617, the Portuguese made an alliance with a group of mercenary raiders called the Imbangala, and in 1618 launched a campaign on Ndongo, invading the kingdom and sacking the capital. This forced Ndongo's king at this time, King Ngola Mbandi, to flee to the island of Kindonga in the Kwanza River. Thousands of Ndongo people were taken prisoner, and the nobles of the Ndongo dynasty were executed.

The Portuguese military campaign of 1618 marched on into neighboring Ndongo ally Matamba and pillaged them, with the help of the mercenary Imbangala. Thousands in Matamba and Ndongo were killed and many more taken as slaves, as the war spilled into the year 1619. The prisoners were made slaves and taken to the slave port in Luanda. There, the enslaved would be baptized, loaded onto slave ships, and then sent to Brazil, New Spain (Mexico), or wherever else in the Americas. Others would be sold to Cairo, Arabia, Turkey, Persia, India, and China.

Which regions did thousands of enslaved in the Kongo come from? One area bordering Kongo was a cartographic region known as *The Land of the Jews,* which bordered the Nile on the East, and the Kingdom of Benin on the West (present-day Southern Nigeria – not present-day Benin). On the other side of the Nile was Abyssinia. Were the people living in the *Land of the Jews* raided and attacked? Were they sold into slavery? Who were they? And who were the enslaved taken from West Africa? (See Chapter 15)

In the previous book, *The Line of Shem and the Seed of Judah*, an ancient prophecy in the first book of the Hebrew Torah was explained. In this journey, three other ancient prophecies from the Hebrew Bible will be examined, dating back thousands of years, and how they will cause us to view the events of 1619 (and 1626) through another lens – a redemptive one. Perhaps even more importantly, will these utterances from the old soothsayers actually come true? Or did they come true already.

On this journey, we will also examine how Slavery started in Colonial America. ***It's not what you think.***

In August 1619, a Spanish slave ship *San Juan Bautista* left Luanda with 350 enslaved souls. Where were they heading? Many more enslaved would follow.

A pitch of darkness engulfed the kidnapped men when the hatch to the hold was dropped, leaving slits of light rays. The men began to feel the big ship's movements, the sensations running against their heads and backs from their positions in the hold.

After several days the men felt certain, after watching the direction of the light from the sun through the slits in the ceiling, that the ship was heading east, then west, then north. Soon they couldn't tell which direction. The air was rank.

The brothers in the hold were yanked from one side to the other as the waves buffeted the slaver. Storm water had sprayed in through the hatch door above them. One of the men, a Hebrew gave a prayer. "O Great Yah, please protect us. O Great YHWH, only you know what our fate will be. Please give unto us faith and endurance. Please forgive us for all our transgressions. If it be Your will, O Yah, please set us free so we can bless your name again. Please remember our families, and remember all on this big canoe who seek your truth."

As the vessel kept charting closer and closer to the land, one of the men chained on deck noted a banner with funny scribble lines making no sense, that to his eyes looked like this:

Point Comfort

As they entered the bay, some of the Congolese men chained on deck were confused when seeing different looking canoes along the banks of the River Congo. The palm trees looked strangely different, yet the tropical heat felt normal. The men also noticed that for some reason the birds looked odd, their singing completely different. One of the Bambara men observed likewise the reaction of the Igbo man, who had been fettered to him this entire crossing, as the man's depressed state of mind fled and his spirit revived when seeing he was back home on the River Niger near Juda. Suddenly, his countenance turned to revulsion when the ship started entering the port and he saw only the white men standing at the landing dock.

The ship was preparing to stop. The men down in the hold felt certain the anchor had now dropped, as the ship slightly keeled and shook on one side. The men could tell the big canoe had landed. The hatch to the hold now opened. Many gave sighs of relief, as fresh air blew in.

The slaver had landed.

CHAPTER 2
1619 and Colonial America

In August 1619, the Spanish slave ship *San Juan Bautista* left Luanda with 350 enslaved Africans and heading towards Vera Cruz. Towards the end of August the ship had crossed Middle Passage, and nearing the coast of Campeche, two English vessels attacked it. One of the privateer ships was called *Treasurer*. The other was called *White Lion*. They stole off of the Bautista about 50 enslaved African persons, who had been captured in the Portuguese wars and held as prisoners at Angola. According to historian Engel Sluiter, Spanish records indicated that on August 30, 1619, *Bautista* ended up delivering only 147 slaves in Vera Cruz, and that it had been robbed by two "corsairs". The records also show that out of thirty-six slave ships landing in Vera Cruz between 1618-1622, *Bautista* was the only one to be attacked.

Both the *Treasurer* and *White Lion* immediately set sail to Colonial Virginia to try to sell the 50 persons for manual labor. The ship *White Lion* arrived at Point Comfort (now Hampton), and according to John Rolfe, the secretary of the Virginia colony, offered "20, and odd Negroes," which were "bought for victualle...at the best and easiest rate they could" by cape merchant Abraham Peirsey, and by the governor Sir George Yeardley. So twenty-some human beings were sold for food.

Treasurer arrived at Point Comfort about three or four days later carrying the rest of the Africans who had been seized, between twenty-five to twenty-nine. The ship captain sold some of them from his illegal seizure, and then set sail to Bermuda to sell the rest.

The twenty-some enslaved from Ndongo, Matamba, Kongo, and other areas within Africa were now in a region completely foreign to them. Many of their fellow ship comrades had died on the way. Many more would soon be coming. Could they survive one year in this unknown environment? No doubt they wanted to return home. The only choice they now had was to learn how to survive.

Slavery in America has been a subject for discussion in tens of thousands of books and forms of literature ever since the word became a part of the English vocabulary. The word and its meaning are embedded in our arts, social culture, and history. Its legacy still affects millions. We probably can safely say its legacy affects everyone in this country today, in one way or another.

One way to fully understand the effect that slavery and its legacy has had, and continues to have, is to look at how it began – just like a person researching their ancestry in order to learn who they are, must first go back and trace the roots of where their family began. And so this book will also trace the beginning of Slavery in America. In 2018, I began a concerted effort to try tracing two family names – Lipscomb and Barnett – by means of conventional genealogy methods and by examining the results of a genetic DNA test. What I discovered would completely shake my whole understanding about race and how Slavery in America was created. If it were not for taking this journey, I would not have been led to the events that started in the year 1619 on the shores of Colonial America.

My great-grandfather said he was a "Black Jew." I will get to that in a minute.

My mother and grandmother, my Grandma Lucy, moved to Oregon from St. Louis, Missouri in 1945. They were moving to re-unite with Grandpapa "Bud," who had come out to Oregon a year earlier when he heard the shipyards were hiring hundreds of laborers. Many people were coming from all across the U.S. for the opportunity to earn better wages. This was during World War II.

My mother was born in Caruthersville, Missouri to Willie and Lucy McCoy. Willie and Lucy came to Caruthersville from Indianola, Mississippi, Lucy's hometown and the place where they were married. I remember in 1989 when first becoming interested in family ancestry – when I started asking my parents and grandparents questions about the family tree. Grandpapa Bud Shelton's family roots took him back to Stuttgart, Arkansas and to Dyersburg, Tennessee, the home of his half Cherokee great-grandmother, Minerva Butler, born in South Carolina, and lived well into her nineties. "My grandfather on my mother's side was Lee Butler, and my grandfather on my dad's side was Richard Shelton, he was from Chattanooga...passed before I was born," said Grandpapa Shelton. I also remember Grandpapa Shelton telling me this: "I was born about 1904...my grandfather Lee Butler was named Butler after the man that owned him...my great-grandfather, Clayton Wilson, he was married to Minerva Butler... they slipped off from the Massa and went over to the Yankee side," during Slavery times and the Civil War.

I couldn't interview my mother's father Willie McCoy, since he had already passed away many years before. Willie and Lucy had a son, Bill McCoy, and another daughter, Doris, who was a teacher for the Hayti Missouri School District. Bill McCoy, after getting out of the U.S. Air Force in Alaska, also moved to Oregon, where he entered politics and became a congressman and State senator. His wife, my Aunt Gladys, also played a prominent role in Oregon history by becoming the first person of African descent to sit on the school board for the Public Schools, and to serve as a County Commissioner.

Willie McCoy was born in Port Gibson, Mississippi, in 1897. "His mother's name was 'Louise Turner' who married a 'Knox,'" my mother said, as she went on to say that Louise died in 1934 at St. Louis. But no one in the family knew anything more about Willie's mother. There were no clues about his father either. Tidbits of information from Willie's baby sister Carrie in Los Angeles, and from other relatives provided some interesting anecdotes about his life. My goal was to trace back as far as possible into the roots of my mother's side of the family.

As the years went by, technology became more advanced in the field of ancestry, and online websites containing databases of genealogy records had became more available than ever. I came across an online database of Missouri death records one day, which renewed my interest in learning about Willie McCoy's mother - "Louise Turner"- who died in St. Louis. To be completely honest, my desire had waned. In previous attempts at researching, I found myself frustrated. First off, I wasn't really all that sure as to how her name came about. Did she first marry Willie McCoy's father and then marry a Turner some time afterward? Or, was her maiden name Turner? Searching the census records over the years to find any documented proof of her existence proved elusive and futile.

I pulled up the Missouri Death Records and entered the name Louise *McCoy*, the year range of 1931-1935, and the city of – St. Louis. Nothing. Trying again, I entered Louise *Turner*, same year range, same city. This time a death certificate for a Louise Turner popped up in St. Louis City, but for the year 1933. Was this her? I examined the record image and made notes, which included a birthplace and names of parents. But was this the right record I was seeking? The birthplace was indeed Mississippi, but how could I verify that this record pertained to my family? Perhaps this was the "Louise Turner" I'd been seeking, and my mother's recollection about Louise passing away in 1934 was just simply a year off. Several days went by, then – I called my Aunt Sue Carolyn in St. Louis and ran the information past her. "Louise Turner married a Knox" I was reminded. The next day I pulled up the website again, and entered "Louise *Knox*." Guess what? Yes, a "Louise Knox" popped up: Colored, widow, died on November 29, 1934 in St. Louis City, Missouri. The death certificate gave her birthdate as January 5, 1876, and listed her parents' names. So my mother's paternal grandmother Louise Turner was no longer a mystery.

What about my mother's people on her maternal side of the family? Her mother – Lucy Lipscomb – was born around 1903 (according to the Census, as no birth record exists) at Indianola, Mississippi to Julius Lucius Lipscomb and Nora Fuller. Lucy's three full siblings were Willie, Robert, and Eddie. Although Lucy's siblings had all passed away when I was coming up, I remember Willie Lipscomb's daughter, who was my Aunt Jessie, her daughter, and her three grandchildren who came out to visit us. I also remembered Eddie Lipscomb's daughter Margaret and her daughter Bobbie. That was during the 1970's.

My grandmother Lucy's father was a minister at a local Baptist church in her hometown. "My father was Julius Lipscomb, born in Columbus, Mississippi," Grandma Lucy said. "My father would write all kinds of poems, songs...he would write speeches for different ones, for their lodge conventions...he would type, had encyclopedias, had a stack, *big* stack." Julius was able to read and write, which explained the sermons and speeches he wrote on a typewriter. Only one of his typed pieces of prose survives, entitled "Victory Triumphant", which my mother carefully preserved. It echoed Great-grandfather Julius' sentiments that Germany be defeated, as it was written at the time of World War I.

According to Mother and Grandmother Lucy, my great-grand-father Julius said he was a "Black Jew." Whether he was making inferences to his true blood ancestry, or voicing socio-political commentary by making historical comparisons between the struggles of blacks and people of Jewish descent, no one in the family knew.

Julius was born in February 1874 in Lowndes County, Mississippi. Twenty years later, in 1894, the young Julius moved to Indianola and met a young widow named Nora Baker. As Julius said in his own words on her obituary that he wrote: "And so modest, and graceful were her deportment, she won his heart and hand in love and she became his loving bride." Grandmother Lucy said of her mother, Nora, "She was born the second year of surrender." She was referring to the second year after the ending of the American Civil War. Nora, whose maiden name was Fuller, was born to Peter and Eliza Fuller on August 6, 1867 at Tibbee Station in Clay County, Mississippi.

Julius and his siblings' father and mother were Julius Sr. and Margaret Lipscomb, who were subjected to life under the inhumane slavery system of America, and working for Dabney Lipscomb, a medical physician and later a state senator, who moved his family and his slaves to Columbus, Mississippi in 1832 from his plantation in Tuscaloosa, Alabama. Julius Lipscomb Sr. was born around 1834 in Columbus, and his wife Margaret, born around 1824 in Georgia. Who were Julius Lipscomb Sr.'s parents? "My father said his grandmother was Leah Dotson," Grandma Lucy said. "My grand-father and my great-grandfather, they were born in slavery, I don't know anything about them." Perhaps Grandma Lucy couldn't tell me anything about them, but she had given me plenty of gold information. She had even given me the name of her father's grandmother – Leah Dotson – which would have been Grandma Lucy's great-grandmother! Could I find a document that could prove this, as well as finding out the name of Grandma Lucy's great-grandfather?

On a trip to the Mississippi State Archives in Jackson, MS during the 1990's, I learned more about Dabney Lipscomb the medical physician, and also of his father, Joel Lipscomb, of Erie, Alabama. Dabney Lipscomb died on June 22, 1850 in Columbus. I requested to look at his estate inventory. Prior to 1865, the Southern slave states considered blacks as mere property – chattel – and therefore black Americans were listed as such on the estate inventories of deceased slave owners. As sad and painful as that fact is, the only consolation to me as a genealogist is the realization that thousands of ancestors are listed by *name, age, and sometimes by family* on such recorded inventories, and thus, the inventories can be a most valuable and powerful reference source for those trying to piece together their family tree when going back into America's slavery era. It proved an invaluable resource for me. Dabney Lipscomb's estate inventory listed seventeen enslaved persons. One of them was a familiar name: – "1 boy, *Julius*, age about 16." This was Julius Lipscomb Sr! His brother Macon was listed with him: "1 negro man, Macon, age about 20." Their brother Gabe was listed too. Also, a girl named Lucy, age about 6. Then I saw this: "1 negro man, Kit, age about 42; 1 negro woman, Leath, age about 42." They were the enslaved parents of slave Julius Lipscomb Sr. So his parents were both born around 1808. After Slavery ended and they received their freedom, Julius and Margaret Lipscomb had children, naming one son and a daughter *Kit and Leah*, born in 1856 and 1860 respectively. There was no question Julius had named two of his children after his parents! Here was my proof. I had no doubt that the couple Kit and Leah listed on the inventory were my Grandma Lucy's great-grandparents.

The archive files in Mississippi showed that the parents of the white slave owner Dabney Lipscomb was Joel Lipscomb, born in Spotsylvania County, Virginia in 1750, and Betsy Chiles, the daughter of William and Agness Chiles. They moved out to Abbeville, South Carolina by 1790 with seven slaves. By 1822, they headed to Greene County, Alabama and settled in the town of Erie, with their enslaved – my ancestors. Grandma Lucy's great-grandfather Kit would have been around fourteen years old. I wondered if Kit's parents came to Alabama with them. Slave owner Joel Lipscomb later died. His estate inventory, dated November 16, 1836, listed thirty-two human beings as property slaves. Were Kit's parents among them? This inventory list did not have their individual ages recorded, but there were age designations – "Man," "Woman," "Child." Separating the children from the adults as best I could, I came up with a list of names: Sam, Daniel and his wife Peg, Seely, Henney, Yellow woman Betty, Omey, Lile, Phillis, Anaka, Rose, and George. Rose and George appeared to be the eldest of the group. The estate appraiser had written "No Value" next to Rose and George's names.

Not seeing Kit and Leah listed, or their children Julius, Macon, Gabe, and Lucy, I realized that they had been taken to Columbus, Mississippi by Dabney Lipscomb. I noticed that two of the enslaved women on the Alabama estate record had names that sounded African –"Omey" and "Anaka." Did my mother's family descend from one of these women, or both? I asked my brother if he had heard anything in the family about this, about being black Hebrew Jews. My brother replied he hadn't heard anything in relationship to that. But he did say he recalled learning there were many black Jews in Africa, and that some had recently immigrated to Israel from Ethiopia.

Did my mother have ancestors who were Hebrew?

CHAPTER 3

More Biblical and Historical References to Hebrew Israelites

Here are a few more biblical and historical facts regarding the original Hebrew Israelites, and of their descendants. Many of these facts are not well known, but they might help you visualize some of the biblical people, culture, and events that occurred in the Levant, as you do your research (For more biblical and historical facts about the Hebrew Jews, see the book, *The Line of Shem & the Seed of Judah*).

The Twelve Tribes of Israel: According to several verses in the first two books of the Torah and of the Old Testament, **the twelve tribes were first formed while they were in "Egypt"** – not during their time in the wilderness or after they entered the Promised Land of Canaan (Genesis 12:34; Exodus 3:28, 29). Another fact often overlooked is that the "Twelve tribes" were a mixture of Semite and Hamite peoples when they were living in Egypt before the Exodus. Israelite men married Egyptian women. Israelite women married Egyptian men. Their offspring became a mixture of the two. Thus, there was "a vast *mixed* crowd" who left Egypt during the exodus who joined alongside the sons of Israel. This *mixed crowd* no doubt also included Egyptian family members who were related to the Israelites and had made a conversion to the worship of Yahuah/Yahweh. We can also keep in mind too, that the word "Egyptian" can also be used as an exonym. So this means that even though many in the Exodus were "Egyptian", some of them might have been ethnically identified as from other parts of Africa, but viewed as Egyptian because they lived in Egypt. Many ancient Egyptians had ancestry from Nubia, Kush/Ethiopia, Sudan, and other regions (Genesis 38:2-5; Genesis 41:45; Exodus 6:13-15; Exodus 12:37,38; See Sources, Chapter 3).

Moses: It is well known, from reading the Torah and the Old Testament, that Moses married Zipporah, who was described as a "Cushite"(Jeremiah 13:23 "Can a Cushite change his skin?"), and also that Moses met her in the land of Midian, which was in NW Arabia. (Exodus 2:16,21; Numbers 12:1) What is often overlooked, however, is that after Moses met the daughters of Reuel at the water well, the daughters came home and told their father Reuel that they had "met an *Egyptian*." (Exodus 2:19) This point may help us visualize what Moses may have looked like. We know that Moses was born in Egypt to Jochabed, who was of the tribe of Levi. This tells us something about Moses' skin tone: his complexion apparently resembled that to some of the Egyptians at that time period. The ancient Egyptians had various skin tones: light-mulatto, brown, and dark, based on their own ancient artwork that has been found.

Phineas, the son of Eleazar: What does the name Phineas, sometimes spelled Phinehas, mean? In the Hebrew Bible are found many personal names of people whose names had a meaning. Some of those meanings are mentioned in the Bible itself, while other meanings can be ascertained from the word language it was written, by the culture and customs, or by the context surrounding the name in which it appears. There are also personal names in the biblical text in which the meanings are not known, or the meaning is in debate due to lack of clarity. So again – Phineas the son of Eleazar and grandson of Aaron the High Priest, what does his name mean, as found in Exodus 6:25?

The Hebrew Bible does not in itself say. In other-words, there is no scripture verse in the Bible or the Torah which literally says what his name means. The meaning of the name is in debate among different scholars and researchers. There seems to be two possible meanings. Some say the name Phineas means, "Mouth of the Serpent/Mouth of Brass." While others say it means, "The Nubian", "the dark-skinned one", or, "the Negro." The name was written in Hebrew in the Torah, and was written by Moses. So why are there two opposite meanings for the name Phineas?

One reason is because the root word of the name originated from a common Egyptian name, and then when Moses transliterated it into Hebrew it became a slightly new name.

Another reason is perhaps due to bias among some research scholars who might be hesitant to (or reject) the idea that Phineas could have been dark-skinned, black.

And another reason, as was stated before, is that the Bible itself does not implicitly state the meaning of his name.

But does the context of the Hebrew Bible, as well as the etymology of the name, give us clues as to which meaning has more weight? Yes.

Let us now explore both meanings of the name Phineas, based on the evidence currently known. We will begin first with the possible meaning,

"Mouth of the Serpent/Mouth of Brass."

To begin, ask yourself, "What possible reason(s) might there be as to why Phineas' name would mean "Mouth of the Serpent"? Could it have a connection perhaps to the account in the Book of Numbers in Chapter 21? This is the account when the Most High told Moses to make a figure in the form of a serpent and place it upon a signal pole so that anyone bitten by the poisonous serpents would survive if they gazed at the brass/copper serpent. Moses did accordingly to

God's instructions. Prior to this event, while the Israelites were wandering in the wilderness, they began to show a rebellious complaining spirit to their circumstances since leaving the land of Egypt. So the Most High punished them by sending poisonous serpents into the camp and many died, until they showed repentance and Moses carried out the instructions for survival.

However, the only problem with this suggestion is that the brass/copper serpent event occurred *After* Phineas was born. In otherwords, Phineas was not named at birth because of the brass/copper serpent event. Phineas was born sometime *before the first plague came upon Pharaoh's Egypt.* Still yet, was Phineas' name prophetic – his couragous loyal action years later when he stopped the "scourge from Yahuah" by grabbing a spear and piercing Zimri and the Midianite Cozbi through her genitals during an immoral sexual encounter right in the midst of Israel's camp? Phineas acted like a "mouth" of a snake, just as a poisonous snake attacks quickly with the deadly bite of its mouth. Even in scripture, the tribe of Dan is prophetically likened to a snake at Genesis 49:17, "Dan shall be a serpent in the way, a viper by the path, that bites the horse's heels so that his rider falls backward." Could it be said that Phineas was a "mouth of brass/copper" in saving Israel?

For his loyal act in not tolerating any uncleanness in Israel's camp, Yahuah/Yahweh made a covenant with Phineas for a lasting priesthood to remain in his ancestral line (until if proven unworthy).

On the other hand, the prophet Jeremiah likened Egypt to a slithering serpent (Jeremiah 46:22), in his pronouncement of judgment upon her, no doubt referring to the pharaohs' practice of wearing their sacred snake headdress as a sign of protection by the serpent-goddess Uatchit. However, it is unthinkable that Eleazar would allow his son's name to carry a meaning connected to idol worship.

The Most High Yehovah commanded that Israel was never to adopt or glorify the false practices of Egypt or any other nation. Now let us examine the other possible meaning of the name Phineas. Then afterward, I will set forth my conclusions.

Phineas: *"The Nubian"/"the dark-skinned one"/"the Negro."* The name was written in Hebrew in the Torah by Moses. The root word of Phineas, *nhsj* originated from a common Egyptian name. When Moses transliterated it from the Egyptian language into the Hebrew language it became a slightly new name when he added the preformative "P" in front of the name as a definite article (See Sources, Chapter 3). Thus, the sounding of the name in Hebrew and the phonetic spelling in English, according to *Strong's Concordance of Hebrew and Greek Words*, would be transliterated as: Piynechac = "Pee-nekh-aws"

In Coptic Egyptian it would be written as: *p3-nhsj*

Written in English: "P-nehesy"

(In Coptic Egyptian the consonant "J" has the sound of "Y")

(See Sources, Chapter 3)

Panehesy, (also spelled Pinehesy), and Nehesy, were common Egyptian names for males. Here are a few examples of documented Egyptians with the name:

Nehesy, Ruler, only reigned 3 days, 14th dynasty, c. 1705 bce

Nehsi, Chief Treasurer of Queen Hatshepsut, 18th dynasty, 1507-1458 bce

Panehesy, Priest at Aten, 18th dynasty, c.1346-1332 bce

Panehsy, Prophet during Ramesses II, 19th dynasty, 1303-1203 bce

Panehesy, Overseer of the Treasuries, 19th dynasty, 1292-1189 bce

Panehesy, Vizier under Merenptah, 19th dynasty, 1213-1203 bce

Panehesy, Viceroy of Kush under Ramesses XI, 20th dynasty, 1189-1077 bce

(See Sources, Chapter 3)

The *Oxford Companion to the Bible*, pg 10, 11 states: "In addition to Hebrew, Greek, and Latin terms for Africa, the Bible also uses Egyptian and Nubian names for the land and its people. From the lower Nile in the North to the upper Nile in the South, the African skin color varied from brown to copper-brown to black. For the Egyptians...the term used for their southern neighbors was Nehesi, "southerner", which eventually also came to mean "the black" or "the Nubian." This Egyptian root (nhsj, with the preformative p" as a definite article) appears in Exodus 6:25 as the personal name of Aaron's grandson, Phinehas (= Pa-nehas)". (See Sources, Ch 3)

Joseph, one of the twelve sons of Jacob, was given an Egyptian name. Phineas' maternal grandfather's name was Puti-el, which was an Egyptian name, hence, notice the root word in his name: *Puti*, which is similar to the Egyptian names of *Poti*-phar and *Poti*-pherah. Here are examples of some names in the Bible and their meaning:

Name:	Meaning in Hebrew:
Ham	Black/Burnt one
Cushi	Ethiopian
Mizriam	Egypt
Moses	Drawn out/saved out of water
Zaphenath-Paneah (Joseph)	Revealer of Hidden Things (and in Egyptian: "God said He will Live!)
Poti-phe-ra	"He whom Ra gave"(Ra – an Egyptian god
Puti-*el*	"He whom *God* gave" (EL = "God")
Misha-el	"Who is like God?"
Uzzi-el	"God is Strength"
El-kanah	"God has Produced"

Other Sources: (See Sources, Chapter 3)

A Hebrew and English Lexicon of the Old Testament, says of Phineas: "Egypt, Pe-nehasi, the Negro"

The Egyptian Origin of Some English Personal Names, Journal of the American Oriental Society:

"The very look of the Hebrew Pi-nehas suggests Ancient Egypt, and it would demand an excessive skepticism to reject the long-accepted derivation from P' –Nhsy "the Nubian.""

Ancient Israel in Sinai: The Evidence for the Authenticity of the Wilderness Tradition:

> "There is no disputing that this word derives from an Egyptian name p3 nhsy, which means "the Nubian." It is not an indicator of ethnicity, but could have been used of a boy of darker complexion."

The past-mentioned references, historical evidence, culture, and scriptural context all lead me to these final conclusions:

> Phineas/Phinehas, the son of Eleazar the Priest of Israel and of an unnamed wife who was the daughter of Putiel, was probably mixed and of dark-skin complexion. Phineas' maternal grandfather Putiel was probably Egyptian, based on the etymology of his name, and he was living in Egypt, where Phineas was born. Although the suggested meaning of Phineas' name, "Mouth of a Serpent/Mouth of Brass" may have been prophetic, both the Torah and the Bible are silent. This suggested meaning might be based on presuming that the name has a Hebrew-only script. Some argue that the "Pi" (or Ph) means "Mouth" and the rest of the name is "nchs" meaning brass/copper. But the root word is not "nchs" but rather "nhsj", as the Hebrew letter used is "Samech", not the Hebrew letter "Shin." Thus, the phonetic sound is of an Egyptian-based name, with the "Pi" (or Ph) definite article to be translated as "the", meaning "the" Nubian, "the" dark-skinned one. However, just like in Joseph's case, the name Phineas might possibly have a dual meaning in Hebrew and in Egyptian.

Further, Nubia was a bordering neighbor to Egypt, being annexed and made a colony of Kemet in the 16ᵗʰ century BCE, becoming identical in culture. Nubians are attested in Egyptian findings as living in Egypt, not to mention of the 25ᵗʰ dynasty of Egypt who were Nubian.

The etymology of the name going far back in Ancient Egyptian history, the culture of Egypt that Phineas was born into, as well as the fact that the Israelites were living among and inter-marrying with "Egyptians" attaches much weight and validity that in fact, Phineas' name did mean "Nubian" and "the dark-skinned one" during that time period in history. Furthermore, adopting this historical evidence does not in any way alter or change the Torah or the Bible's message that a Messiah would one day come who would be of the "Tribe of Judah" as prophesied. Who is the foretold Messiah supposed to be? Did he already come, or something yet future? What actually did the ancient prophets say? We will examine this in Chapters 12 & 13.

Eber, the great-grandson of Shem and forefather of Abraham:

His name has the root meaning, *"Pass over/cross," or "Other side, opposite side."* At Genesis 10:21, Shem (a Son of Noah) is spoken of as "the forefather of all the sons of *Eber*." Eber's name appears at Numbers 24:24, and applies Eber's name either to a certain people or a certain region centuries after his death, and seems to be referring to the land or people *on the other side* of the Euphrates River. In Hebrew the expression *"Beyond the river"* is used several times in the Bible to refer to the region west of the Euphrates. (Nehemiah 2:7,9; 3:7)

The term "*Hebrew*" seems to comes from the name *Eber* ('E'ver). The Greek Septuagint, the Syriac Peshitta, and the Latin Vulgate all render the name "Eber" as "*the Hebrews.*"

In my previous book, several ethnic peoples living in West Africa are cited who are Hebrew Jews. Here is another group: the Ewe, or Eve people, a population of ten million living in Ghana, Togo, and Benin. They believe they are also the descendants of Eber. Just as in the Hebrew language the second alphabet letter "Bet" can have a phonetic sound of "V" or "B", the "Eve" people say their name has the root word of Eber. The Eve or Ewe's oral story about their migration into West Africa says they originated in **Canaan** and then migrated to Egypt, then to Khartoum, then to a land not far from Khartoum called "Seme", and then across the Sahel into "Ketu" by the 1500's, a town now in the country of Benin. Some of the customs of the Eve is that they practice male circumcision on the 8th day; a man can inherit his deceased brother's wife to produce offspring in the deceased brother's name (similar to what was practiced by the Israelites); and they commemorate annually the Israelites' Exodus from Egypt. Finally, another fascinating fact about them is the meaning of their Ewe word "Togo" which means *On the other side of the river.*" (More about the Ewe people in Chapter 15)

The Land of Canaan "in Egypt" by the Mediterranean Sea:

We know the boundaries of Africa today are not the same as in ancient Africa. For example, we know the modern term "Middle East" was not used by Abraham, Joseph, ancient Egypt, nor by anyone in the entire Bible. So what was the region "Middle East" originally called? Immediately after the global flood, Noah and his family left the Ark in the Ararat Mountain range of Turkey/Armenia and migrated to an area between the Tigris and Euphrates rivers which came to be called Shinar. After the Tower of Babel incident, a mass migration headed into the area known later as Kemet, from which Egypt arose as the first world power of Bible prophecy. So the region which many today refer to as the "Middle East" was originally under the suzerainty of Egypt centuries before Abraham crossed the Euphrates.

The Bible records that Ham (son of Noah) had four sons. One of them was Canaan, whose descendants were the Canaanites. The Canaanites settled in area near the Mediterranean Sea which came to be called the "Land of Canaan." According to the Bible, the boundaries of the land of Canaan "came to be from Sidon as far as Gerar, **near Gaza**, as far as Sodom and Gomorrah and Admah and Zeboiim, near Lasha." The ancient city of Gaza is still in existence to this day on the Mediterranean Coast (despite the current news of horrific war and occupation). <u>The city of Gaza became a land bridge which connected to Egypt</u>. Whether the descendants of Canaan migrated to this land directly after the Tower of Babel incident or whether they migrated first to Kemet and then to the land of Canaan, the Bible does not say (Genesis 10:6, 15-19).

In the 20th Century BCE, Abraham and his wife Sarah left their home of Ur, crossed the Euphrates River and settled in the land of Canaan. Years after Abraham and Sarah's death, their grandson Jacob continued to dwell in the land of Canaan with his twelve sons. His son Joseph was sold into slavery by his jealous brothers and taken to Egypt where he was thrown into prison. While in prison, Joseph said to the chief cupbearer, **"I was kidnapped from the land of the Hebrews."** Thus, the land of Canaan came to also be known as the *"Land of the Hebrews."* (Genesis 37: 1-28; 40:15)

The land of Canaan or land of the Hebrews (which later became the territory of the Twelve Tribes of Israel) **was located without question along the Mediterranean Sea. This is proven by the discov-**

ery of the **Amarna Tablets and the granite stela of Egyptian King Merneptah.** In 1898 archaeologists found in a temple at Thebes a black granite pillar that boasts of the achievements of Egyptian King Merneptah of the 19th Dynasty, believed to have reigned in the late 13th Century BCE. Inscribed on the stela are these words: "Israel is laid waste, his seed is no more." This is the only known reference to the nation of Israel in ancient Egyptian texts thus far, and the earliest reference to Israel outside the Bible. The stela was made during the period of the Judges, the time period right after the Israelites under Joshua entered the land of Canaan and divided the land into twelve territories. Over time, the land of Canaan was also called Judea.

In 70 CE, the Roman armies destroyed Jerusalem's temple in Canaan, and Hebrew Jews were scattered to Africa and other parts of the Roman Empire. After the second Jewish revolt between 132-135 CE, the Romans banned the Hebrews from entering the city of Jerusalem for nearly two centuries, and the province of Judea was renamed *Syria Palaestina* in an attempt to get rid of the name Judea.

Ancient Prophecies that Hebrew Israelites would become Slaves:

In the Book of Deuteronomy, Chapter 28, the Most High God mentioned what would happen to the Israelites if they did not obey His commandments – they would become slaves again.

In the Book of Luke, Chapter 21, verse 24, it states of the Jews, whose temple would later be destroyed by the Romans in 70 ce: And they will fall by the edge of the sword *and be led captive into all the nations*…until the appointed Times of the Gentiles are fulfilled."

In the Book of Isaiah, Chapter 11, verse 12 prophesied that the "scattered" anointed ones of Judah "will be gathered together from the *four corners* of the earth."

Would not the four corners of the Earth be: Africa, Europe, Asia and the Islands, **and the Americas?**

Yeshua/Yahshua:

There are so many, many texts in the Bible that refer to Yeshua/ Yahshua, the name when translated into Spanish/Latin is "Jesus/ Hesus." Let us focus on two particular texts about Yeshua/Jesus found in the second half of the Bible, namely the Greek Scriptures (or commonly called the New Testament). These two texts have been the subject of much interest and discussion. Why? Because these texts seem to provide a description of Jesus' physical appearance. Here are the texts which are causing much interest:

> "And in the midst of the lampstands someone like a son of man…His head and his hair were white, **as white wool**, as snow…**and his feet were like fine copper when glowing in a furnace**." (Revelation 1:13 – 15)

> "These are the things that the Son of God says, the one who has eyes like a fiery flame **and whose feet are like fine copper**." (Revelation 2:18)

The first verse calls Yeshua/Yahshua the "Son of man," a term appearing often in the Gospels, which Yeshua applied to himself. The verse then states his hair was white. This obviously is referring to "Wisdom," just as that phrase means similarly to aged persons, as a sign of the acquired "wisdom" they have gained over their many years of life.

But what do the verses mean when it says that Yeshua/Yahshua's hair was as white "wool" and his feet like "fine copper"? Why did Yeshua tell the apostle John to write the word *wool*? John could have said Yeshua's hair was as white snow, or white fabric/clothing, or as white cotton. But he said white **wool**. Does this seem to imply *hair texture*?

Some have suggested the mention of wooly hair is referring to Jesus as being the "Lamb of God," symbolizing the sacrifice Yahshua gave of himself, just as the Hebrew High Priest of Levi had to offer a physical lamb for the sins of the Israelite people. This phrase "Lamb of God" occurs in the Book of Revelation 28 times. However, that phrase does not appear in the text under consideration. *Is the mention of wooly hair referring to one of Jesus' human features when he was a man?* The mention of wooly hair in historical literature most often than naught refers to a person of dark complexion or a descendant of a dark complexioned person or people. We have already noted that the Israelites and the Egyptians intermarried. But even going further back, one of the sons of Shem was Asshur, the forefather of the Assyrians. How are the Assyrians depicted in carved reliefs? As physically strong, dark-complexioned, heavy eyebrows and beard, and prominent nose. It is interesting to note, too, that according to the Gospel account of Matthew, when King Herod issued the order to have all the Hebrew male babies from two years and under killed, an angel told Joseph to take the infant Jesus and "flee to Egypt." Might this be an indication of Jesus being of dark complexion – he would blend in with that part of the Egyptian population who were dark complexioned? (Matthew 3:13-15)

Eliezer Ben Hurcanus, or Hycanus (80 - 118 CE), is considered one of the most prominent sages of the 1st and 2nd Centuries in Judea. He was a member of the Sanhedrin. Today in Jewish rabbinic readings, Hurcanus' writings are still read. One of his works is the midrash entitled "Pirkei DeRabbi Eliezer" (Chapters of Rabbi Eliezer), which is traditionally ascribed to Hurcanus and was edited in the 8th or 9th century CE. In Chapter 24, entitled *Nimrod And The Tower Of Babel* it says this:

"Noah brought his sons and his grandsons, and he blessed them with their settlements, and he gave them as an inheritance all the earth. **He especially blessed Shem and his sons, dark but comely,** and he gave them the habitable earth. He blessed Ham and his sons, dark like the raven, and he gave them as an inheritance the coast of the sea. He blessed Japheth and his sons, them entirely white, and he gave them for an inheritance the desert and its fields; these which he endowed them."

In later years of his life, Eliezer Ben Hurcanus was quoted as saying "I have never taught anything which I had not learned from my masters."

Next, the texts say that Jesus' feet were like fine "copper." Other Bible translations say "like fine brass" or "like fine bronze." Copper, a chemical element, when compounded with tin, creates the alloy bronze. Brass is similar to bronze, composed of copper and zinc, and described as yellow or gold. Pure copper has been described as reddish-gold, pinkish-orange, red-orange. When exposed to air, oxidized copper becomes brown-black. We have seen this when comparing a new copper penny to an old one.

Some have said that humans do not look like the color of pure copper. Perhaps. What then about oxidized copper? Interestingly, people who are not familiar with the history of Slavery or with Slavery records, do not realize that many enslaved persons were described as "yellow" or as "copper-colored." Consider the case that went up to the Supreme Court of Virginia in 1827, "Gregory vs. Baugh," in which a black man named "James Baugh, a man of color...brought an action against Thomas Gregory to recover his freedom. The court case continued, "the plaintiff [Baugh] proved by two witnesses that he is the son of Biddy, who was the daughter of Sibyl; that Sibyl was **a copper-colored woman**, with straight black hair, with the general appearance of an Indian, except that she was too dark to be of the whole blood; that she was called Indian Sibyl, but her color, and that only, shewed she had Negro blood."

Here is another case. In the Supreme Court of Louisiana, a bill of sale was presented as evidence, which read: "Be it known that on this twenty-fifth day of March in the year 1830...personally came appeared, Richard Walter Long of Tiffin County, of Tennessee...in consideration of three hundred and fifty dollars cash...bargain, sell, and deliver...a Negro named Absalom, aged about fourteen years, **of a copper colored**, or grifl'e, a slave for life."

There are hundreds of examples like this found in Slavery documents.

Samuel Stanhope Smith, a minister and the seventh president of Princeton University from 1795 to 1812, said about the Jews: "They are...brown in France and in Turkey, swarthy in Portugal and Spain...**tawny or copper-colored in Arabia and Egypt**."

Jesus' feet is described as like fine copper/bronze/brass. In scripture, "Gold" symbolizes heavenly things, whereas "Copper" symbolizes *"earthly things."* So again, just as with the mention of wooly hair – is the reference to "Copper" pointing to Jesus' human features when he was a man? Yahshua referred to himself as the *"Son of man."*

It is only natural to want to learn what Yeshua/Yahshua looked like when he was alive on earth. The Most High will surely reveal more, when and if He chooses to. In the meantime, continue to research the people, culture, and lands of biblical events. Visualize Bible scenes as you understand them with true facts.

African Slave Traders Traveling to a Slave Market

BURNING OF A VILLAGE IN AFRICA, AND CAPTURE OF ITS INHABITANTS.

Burning of a Village in Africa and Capture of its Inhabitants

Sig. 226. Sklaventransport in Afrika.

African Slaves transport

The Capture of Slaves

Slaves Waiting for Sale – Richmond

Slave Hunt, Dismal Swamp

Drummer at Hamed

Women at Kotel

Arab Women in Jerusalem carrying containers filled with Labaneh

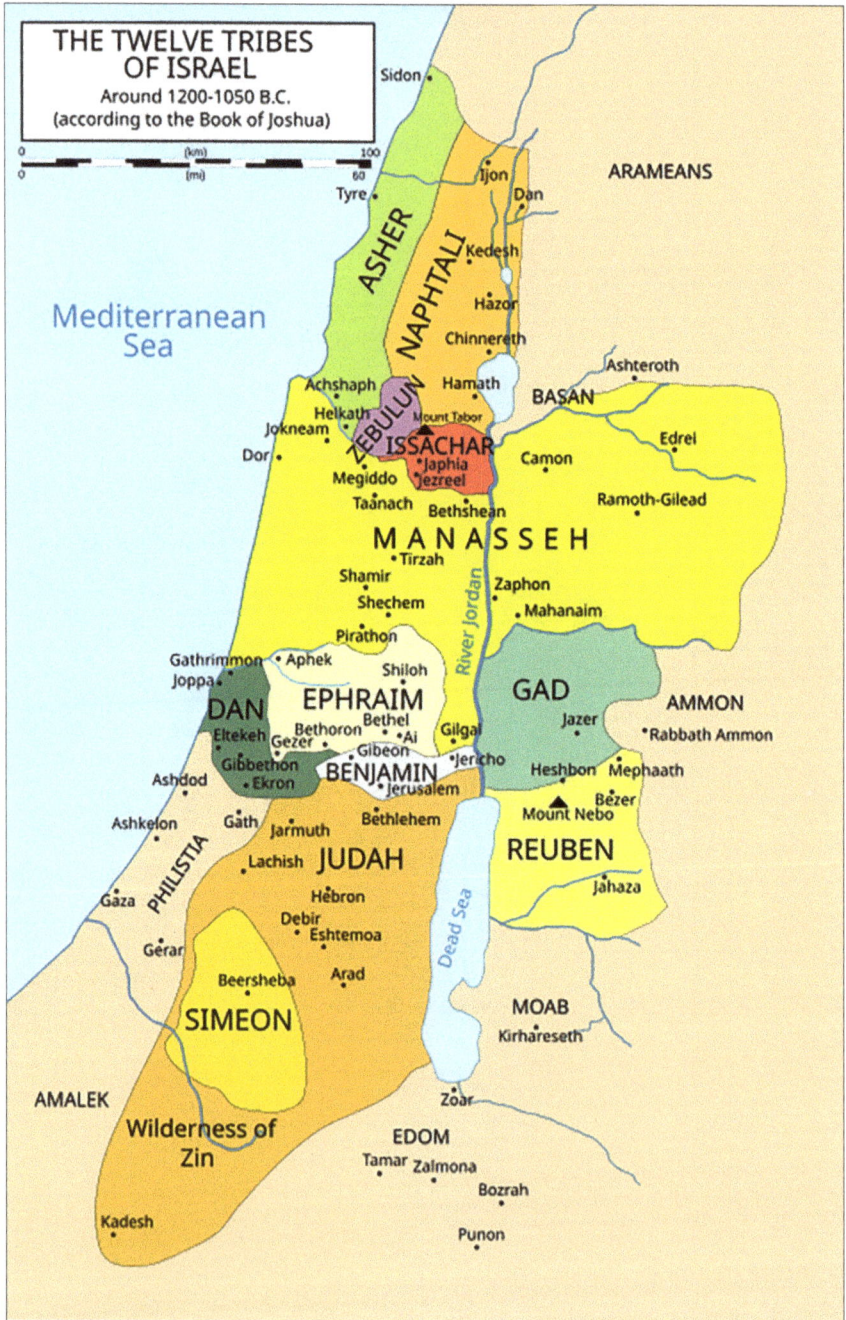

THE TWELVE TRIBES OF ISRAEL
Around 1200-1050 B.C.
(according to the Book of Joshua)

12 Tribes of Israel

CHAPTER 4

Maybe They Were Never Slaves

To see the estate inventories of Dabney Lipscomb and Joel Lipscomb, showing the names of human beings of African descent and listing them as nothing more than mere chattel or real estate property, is a horrific experience. To also know that those persons listed were your own ancestors, can find oneself with a loss for words. That pain goes not only for the descendants of the enslaved, but also for the descendants of the enslaver. A healing needs to take place for both sides.

Those inventories were taken in 1836 and 1850. The first inventory was taken five years after the 1831 Slave "uprising" of Nat Turner. The other inventory was taken both after Nat Turner and the 1839 *Amistad* court victory. How does one reconcile calling one event a Victory, but the other event an uprising, a rebellion, a revolt? To this day, the well-known failed struggles for freedom that occurred in this nation's history during Slavery are still referred to as "Insurrections", "Revolts", "Uprisings", "Rebellions." Then after Reconstruction came Jim Crow and the tragedies of Tulsa and Rosewood. Again, as was stated in the beginning of this book, Slavery, and its legacy, can better be understood by understanding how it began. After such an investigation, can then the healing begin.

Although Grandmother Marcella and I never met, I'm certain she would have been a wonderful grandmother to me. She passed away before I was born. She raised my father with all the love in the world. Marcella married Hugh Hanks, in 1922 in Manhattan, Kansas. She was born Marcella Barnett on December 25, 1898 in Ogden, Kansas. There is only one photograph in the family that exists of Marcella and Hugh. Although Marcella was not able to meet her grandchildren in Oregon, her two surviving sisters did, Aunt Valjeen and Aunt Peggy. According to my memory, they came out to visit at least two or three times during the summer months when my brothers and I were growing up. They would board the train from Kansas to Oregon and back. Aunt Valjeen and Aunt Peggy brought their love when they came. They also brought Grandmother Marcella's warm love and affection too.

I wish that I could interview all three of them today, and learn more about my paternal grandmother's family, the Barnetts. But all of them are now long gone. Grandmother Marcella passed in 1952. Aunt Valjeen passed away in 1978. She had been a Blues entertainer in Manhattan, Kansas, performing the popular "boogie woogie" sound as a singer and piano player at the local music clubs. The last one to go, Aunt Peggy, passed away in 1990 just a few months before I was planning to come visit her.

Marcella Barnett's parents were married on June 8, 1885 in Ogden, Kansas – Benjamin Barnett and Gertrude Jane Green. How far back could I stretch into Grandmother Marcella's roots? Starting with her mother, Gertrude Green, my great-grandmother, she was born March 10, 1871 in Lawrence, Kansas, six years after the American Civil War, to Pitt "Green" Gaines and Harriett Alexander Gaines. Gertrude's baby sister Mayme Stemons came along by May of 1873. Gertrude's mother Harriett Alexander came to Lawrence, Kansas from Kentucky, along with Harriett's mother Mary Parris. Gertrude's father, Pitt "Green" Gaines was born around 1844 in

Platte City, Missouri to unknown parents, slaves on the plantation of Richard P. Gaines of Saint Joseph, Missouri, according to Pitt's pension papers.

Apparently, Pitt Gaines somehow made it off the plantation and enlisted with Company C, of the Kansas Colored Volunteers, on the 8th of July 1863. Pitt experienced the fray of battle. On April 18th, 1864, Confederate forces at the battle of Poison Spring, Arkansas captured and killed many of the First Kansas Colored Regiment. The men of the Second Regiment had vowed revenge.

On the afternoon of April 29, 1864 the Union forces, including Company C of the Kansas Colored Volunteers, reached Jenkins Ferry, Arkansas and began building a pontoon bridge to cross the Saline River. The men began marching along Saline Bottom, a two-mile-wide expanse on both sides of Saline River. Union forces tried to cross Saline Bottom as it turned into a sea of mud due to heavy rain. The Confederate forces arrived on the 30th and an exchange of military fire took place. The Union soldiers, including black soldiers, repulsed the attacks and finally crossed the river with wounded men and supply wagons. Many supply wagons eventually were abandoned in the swamp north of Saline. Many of the most seriously wounded Union soldiers were left behind. Dozens of other wounded Union soldiers were moved to hospitals, where many succumbed to their wounds.

During the battle the Second Colored became the first black Union soldiers to successfully capture a Confederate field artillery battery. The Union loss was heavy: 64 killed, 378 wounded, 86 captured and missing. While helping to remove two pieces of artillery captured in the fight at Saline Bottom, Pitt Gaines was caught between the gun caisson and a limber carrying the artillery ammunition, and the shifting weight crushed his left hip. He was removed to a hospital where he remained some three months.

The Kansas Colored Volunteers merged into the 83rd Regiment of the United States Colored Troops (USCT), Infantry, and Gaines was discharged October 9th, 1865, at Leavenworth, Kansas. Pitt was grateful to not have been severally wounded and left at the battle scene to die, or that he had not succumbed to his wounds at the hospital. But he carried his injury for the rest of his life. Receiving his service pension during his later years, Pitt "Green" Gaines eventually passed away in 1915, leaving his two married daughters Gertrude Green Barnett and Mayme Stemons. According to the *Osage County Herald* newspaper, Pitt Gaines was supposed to have "left considerable money hidden out somewhere in gas pipes & tin cans." The article concluded, "And a search will be made for it." Perhaps that was how the name "Green" became attached to Pitt Gaines' name. I never found out whether any money had been found. If the story was true, hopefully Pitt's daughters were able to get their hands on it.

Benjamin Barnett, named after his father, was born in 1865 at Eudora, Kansas, right soon after his parents and hundreds of other families during 1863 had crossed the Missouri River and fled from their slave masters across the river in Missouri. All of Benjamin's five older siblings had been born in Missouri between 1855-1862: Charles, Elsie, James, Frances, or "Fannie," and Garrett. Some families escaped slavery and came into Kansas by means of the "Underground Railroad," while other families – such as Pitt "Green" Gaines – saw Union Army soldiers passing by their plantations and decided to make a run for it and join their military units for protection and a safe passage out of Slavery.

Benjamin Barnett Sr. purchased a farm by 1870. The farm contained 200 acres, 5 acres of winter wheat, 25 acres of corn, and 1 acre of sorghum. The real estate of the farmland was valued about $2000. Some of the Barnett's neighboring black farming families were the

Nortons, Hendersons, Colemans, Harris, Ray, Perkins, Bass, and Gibsons, among others.

In time, the Barnett children left the family farm and ventured out in the world to start families of their own. Fannie Barnett got married to a man named Edwards in 1878. Elsie Barnett also found a husband, later having children and grandchildren. Their brother James married a daughter from the Ray family in 1875. Benjamin Barnett Jr. moved over to Riley County and married Gertrude Green. Charles traveled further, to Superior Township in Osage County, and found his bride.

So who were Benjamin and Jane Barnett - the parents who bravely crossed over the border with their children from the slave State of Missouri and into the free State of Kansas in 1863? Who were their ancestors?

According to Federal Census records, Benjamin Barnett, the father, was born about 1835, and wife Jane, born around 1840. Both stated they were born in Virginia, *as well as their parents*. Based on the age of their first child Charles, Benjamin and Jane formed their marital bond around 1854. Five of their children were born in Missouri before coming to Kansas, and seems to have been from Marshall, Missouri in Saline County, where their daughter Elsie was born. The patriarch Benjamin Barnett eventually died sometime between 1880 and 1900. His widow Jane Barnett then moved in with her daughter Elsie in Ottawa, Kansas, until Jane's death in 1924.

Did Benjamin and Jane get escorted into Kansas in 1863 by means of a Union Army unit? Several Union Army troops were freeing people from slave plantations in Missouri during the Civil War. Many others freed themselves, escaping from slave-owning plantations, heading to safe havens in Kansas, and courageously braving the odds of recapture by the "paddy wagons." The "Underground

Railroad" was also providing secret escape routes from slave masters and slave catchers.

The National Archives held records of pension payments to Civil War Veterans. One of the records was on a "Benjamin Barnett" who was a Civil War soldier with the 79th United States Colored Volunteers Infantry. A pension payment had been made in 1923 to his beneficiary "Jane Barnett." This former soldier Private Benjamin Barnett had enlisted with the 79th United States Colored Troops on November 2nd, 1863 at Waldrum, Arkansas. He was described as 28 years of age, five feet, ten inches, complexion black, occupation Farmer, and born in the Creek Nation. This soldier's age in 1863 matched my ancestor's age of the same name. The soldier, a private in Company I, had a beneficiary named "Jane Barnett", also similar to my ancestor. Was Grandmother Marcella's grandfather born in the Creek Nation and therefore was part Native Creek Indian? Private Benjamin Barnett was later admitted to a hospital at Fort Gibson in October of 1864. Then he was mustered out of the service at Pine Bluff, Arkansas on October 1, 1865. According to the records, former private Benjamin had become an invalid later in life. The beneficiary payment went to his wife Jane Barnett at an address in Oklahoma in 1923. Did Grandmother Marcella have family members living in Oklahoma? Did her grandmother Jane live there for a minute before she passed away in Kansas in 1924?

My curiosity was peeked over the top. I pulled up the 1920 Federal Census for Oklahoma in the county for the town listed in the soldier records, and there I located Private Benjamin's wife Jane Barnett. Not only that, Private Benjamin was still alive and living with his wife at their home. Just as I was starting to get excited, I realized my mistake. This Benjamin and Jane Barnett were both listed as being born in Oklahoma. Clearly, this was not Grandmother

Marcella's grandparents, as Marcella's grandmother Jane Barnett was living in Ottawa, Kansas with her daughter Elsie that same year. Glad I had caught my error in mistaken identity before I had gone way too far on this journey. May that be a lesson to all my kindred genealogists searching their ancestry. Make sure to verify, and re-verify, all your "discoveries" before proceeding further.

After that reality check, I asked myself – how did my ancestors end up in Missouri? I had assumed a slave owner brought them to Missouri as slaves. But was I correct in *assuming* that as fact? Maybe they were never slaves. Maybe they were *free persons of color.*

Benjamin Barnett seemed to be related to another farmer named James Barnett, another person who had come to Kansas with his wife and children by 1865. James Barnett, born around 1833, had testified as a witness in a divorce proceeding in 1877 involving one of Benjamin Barnett's sons. Something else was notable about the two men, Benjamin Barnett and James Barnett – they both had a son named Charles. Also, Benjamin Barnett had another son, named James, and James Barnett had another son, Benjamin. Benjamin listed both his parents as natives of Virginia. James listed his mother a native of Virginia, and his father from Kentucky.

Benjamin Barnett and James Barnett were very possibly brothers. The fact that James Barnett was asked to testify for another black man whose last name was the same, *in another County*, was strong circumstantial evidence that the two men, Benjamin and James, were related. They also both had sons named after the other, and both had sons named Charles. **Were the sons named after ancestors?**

I needed also to establish whether both men had come to Missouri as slaves or as free persons. None of their names showed up as "Free Persons of Color" on the census records for Missouri prior to 1870. Nor could I determine if any plantation owner had brought them to Missouri. Not having much to go on, I narrowed my search for slave owners with the last name of Barnett in two Missouri counties – Saline and Lafayette. I picked Saline County because that was where Benjamin's daughter Elsie was born. I then chose Lafayette County because it held the largest slave population in Missouri by the eve of the Civil War. Lafayette was Missouri's leader in hemp production. Hemp rope was in high demand, as it was used to tie cotton bales. So hemp was the principal product in Lafayette, and Lafayette was the leader in slavery bondage in the state.

There were a few candidates who could have perhaps brought Benjamin, and possibly even his wife Jane, to Missouri. But without documents that showed me proof, it was just speculation at that point. Without coming across more records to examine, the feeling of frustration began to creep in. Would a DNA test perhaps help?

If Benjamin were a free person of color, it was doubtful he would have headed to a Slave state. On the other hand, there were many accounts of free persons of color who had been kidnapped by slave catchers and sold into Slavery! So that was a possibility too. Nothing could be ruled out as yet. Since Benjamin had said he was born around 1835, and he and Jane's first child, Charles, was born about 1855, could there be found land owners named Barnett who lived in Virginia around the 1840 time period, but who then moved to Missouri by the 1850's? That strategy didn't quite produce the grand result I had hoped, but it did get me to start thinking outside the box. I went to the Internet and started searching "Benjamin Barnett, Negro slave in Virginia" while adding a different Virginia county name in each search attempt, seeing what might come up. I was fishing, experimenting. Then one day I tried something different.

On this particular day I tried a search with the key words, "Charles Barnett, Negro slave in Virginia." I had decided to try this approach, since Benjamin and Jane named their first son Charles. A nagging thought for quite some time was that "Charles" might have been named after an ancestor, perhaps the name of a grandparent or great-grandparent. That is a common search rule in Genealogy. Family names are passed down and repeated through succeeding generations of descent. As I entered my key search words, a result came up, taking me to the court records of Albemarle County, Virginia and saying the following:

"Feb 14, 1746 Ordered that the children of Mary Barnett – Charles, Lettice, Ned, Frances, and William be by the Church wardens in this County severally Bound out."

Based on past genealogy experience, I knew this court entry probably had to do with a white woman giving birth to mixed children by a black man who was probably enslaved. I went to the website that cited the source document and read two more Virginia Court records pertaining to this woman, stating that she would be bound out for five years more in Spotsylvania County after her original term of Indenture ends:

"Mary Barnett for having a mulatto bastard by a Negro man servant of Edwin Hickman, Oct 2, 1728."

"Mary Barnett a christian white woman servant belonging to Mr. Edwin Hickman for having a bastard Mulatto Child, Nov. 4, 1730."

I was fascinated by the information I had stumbled across. A white female indentured servant and a black male servant – both servants of an Edwin Hickman – had produced mixed children, *and one of the children was a boy named Charles.* I had to research this event more. What happened to the boy Charles? Did he survive to adulthood and take his mother's surname Barnett? Did he later go to Saline County, Missouri? I would only hope.

So who was Edwin Hickman? Born in 1690, Edwin Hickman was the Sheriff of Spotsylvania County, Virginia during 1729-1730 and later of Albemarle County, Virginia. He married twice, his first wife being Elender Webber Chiles, <u>widow of John Chiles of Spotsylvania County, who (surprisingly to me) was the great-grandfather of Betsy Lipscomb, who, along with her husband Joel Lipscomb, had enslaved my Grandma Lucy's great-great-grandparents Kit and Leah Lipscomb</u> (as discussed in Chapter 2). In 1734, Edwin Hickman obtained a land patent with three other men for 3277 acres in Albemarle County, and moved there with his wife Elender and their servants. Two of those servants were an unnamed black male and a White indentured servant named Mary Barnett, who gave birth to two mulatto boys and was punished by Hickman for doing so.

After serving as Sheriff, Hickman later was appointed as Justice of the Peace around 1744. Edwin Hickman was neighbor to Peter Jefferson, the father of future President Thomas Jefferson. Hickman was a witness to the Last Will & Testament of Peter Jefferson.

On February 4, 1758, Edwin Hickman prepared and signed his Last Will & Testament (he did not die until 1769), mentioning by name, eight "NEGRO" servants: two women – Dinah and Alice; Three girls – Muteller, Alley, and Grace; and three boys – Ben, Charles, and David.

It was in the realm of possibility that the boy named Charles in Edwin Hickman's Will, was Mary Barnett's son Charles mentioned in the 1746 court order to be bound out. If that were true, then in the year the Will was signed, 1758, Charles would have been at least twelve or thirteen years of age. [On a side note, after Edwin Hickman's death, most of his 3277 acres bequeathed to his sons later became what is now the city of Charlottesville, Virginia].

Were there any records of a "Charles Barnett" in Albemarle County after Edwin Hickman's death? On September 18, 1780, there was a Charles Barnett who enlisted in Charlottesville with the 7th Virginia Regiment during the American Revolution. His enlistment application stated he was age 18, five feet, five inches, of yellow complexion, and born in Albemarle County. Then on September 7, 1785, there was a marriage entry in Albemarle County to *Lucy Bowles, a Free Person of Color* born around 1765, and Charles Barnett. In 1787, this same Charles Barnett purchased 40 acres from William Johnson, who owned land adjacent to Thomas Jefferson and the deceased Edwin Hickman. Charles' mother-in-law Amy Bowles Farrow, *a Free Person of Color*, would purchase 224 acres of land from William Johnson the following year, 1788.

By January 3, 1791, Charles Barnett was a bondsman to the marriage of Richard Brock and Mary Goin, daughter of Benjamin Goin, who consented to the marriage. *Benjamin Goin was a Free Person of Color.* Then on August 2, 1796, a "Charles Barnett" registered as a Free Man of Color: "A dark mulatto man aged about thirty years, of a yellow complexion, five feet seven and three quarters high, having proved to the satisfaction of this Court that he was *born a free man within this County.*" The court gave Charles a Certificate of Freedom.

Clearly, there were at least two, maybe three persons, who took the name "Charles Barnett" in Albemarle County, Virginia between 1746 and 1796. The Revolutionary War application and the Certificate of Freedom registration seemed certain to have been the same person, given the ages on both documents pointed to a birth date between 1762 and 1766. Not much of a discrepancy. But the "Charles" named in Edwin Hickman's Will in 1758, and Mary Barnett's child "Charles" being bound out by the court in 1746, did not seem to be "Free man of Color and soldier" Charles Barnett. *Unless he had lived to be a hundred, or more.* It wasn't impossible, just unlikely. Unless there was a document to show otherwise (See Chapter 17).

The original question – who were my Barnett ancestors and how did they end up in Missouri from Virginia – was still unanswered. Also, were Benjamin and Jane's son Charles *named after an ancestor?* Learning about the Barnetts of Albemarle County, Virginia and all the other Free Persons of Color in that community had made me begin to think – *how did they become free?*

Maybe they had never been slaves.

CHAPTER 5

The DNA Test Results

Because of the growing popularity in taking a DNA test for genealogical purposes, I finally decided to take mine. A genealogical DNA test looks at specific locations of a person's genome, in order to find or verify ancestral genealogical relationships and/or to estimate the ethnicity of an individual. A **genome** is the **genetic material** of an organism consisting of DNA, or **Deoxyribonucleic acid,** a molecule composed of two chains that coil around each other to form a double helix carrying the genetic instructions used in the growth, development, and reproduction of all known living organisms. Three principal types of genealogical DNA tests are available, with each looking at a different part of the genome and useful for different types of genealogical research. The three principal types of genealogical tests are autosomal (tracing both male and female lines), mitochondrial **or mtDNA** (tracing the mother's line from mother to child), and **Y chromosome or** Y-DNA, (tracing the father's line from father to son). Only males can take the Y-DNA tests, because only males have a Y-chromosome. If you are a female and wish to determine your direct paternal DNA ancestry, you can ask your father, brother, paternal uncle or his son (your cousin), or paternal grandfather, to take the test for you.

We all have 23 chromosomes. The Autosomal tests look at chromosomes 1–22 and X, which are inherited from both parents and all recent ancestors. Both males and females receive an X-chromosome from their mother, but only females receive a second X-chromosome from their father.

All humans descend in the direct female line from the Mitochondrial Eve, a female originating in Africa (and perhaps an Africa much wider than the current boundaries we know today). Some say Eve lived around 200,000 years ago. Others say she lived about 6,000 years ago. The Bible's chronology (in the Book of Genesis) also points to a 6,000 year time period. Different branches of her descendants are called **haplogroups**, representing the major branches of the human family tree.

I took my test in August 2011 and got my results back the next month, showing well over one thousand other DNA tested persons who were related to me genetically. The profiles were listed in the order of closest relative and down to the least close relative, based on the percentage amount of shared DNA. Right at the top of the list were my two Lipscomb cousins on my mother's side of the family. They were descended from one of Grandma Shelton's brothers – her brother Eddie Lipscomb. This immediately told me that my test was genuine. Of course, if my two cousins had not taken the test with the same company that I had, then they obviously would not have shown up. Out of all of these one thousand-plus names, my two cousins were the only people I knew. The rest of them were completely unknown. Some of them were at the top of the list, meaning they were *closely* related to me. So now it would be up to each one of them and myself to figure out *HOW* we were related. There were also cousins listed who were related to my father's side of the family.

My test results revealed I was 83% African, roughly 18% European, and 1% Native American. My European ancestry was made up of British, Irish, Scandinavian, and populations by the Mediterranean Sea. The Native American results also included SE Asian ancestry from populations of Thai, Khmer, Indonesian, and Myanmar. That was a surprise. The largest part of my ancestry, about eighty-three percent, came from West Africa, including Nigeria, Ghana, Benin/Togo, Congo, and several other regions.

Another feature of the DNA website was the ability to send messages to my matches and correspond with them, as well as seeing the names of each other's matches that we shared. I began sending messages to several persons whose profiles listed surnames that were in my family lines. After sending messages to my genetic cousins, some would kindly reply, sharing their vital records with me. But none of us could identify who were the ancestors we shared in common, or how our family trees had become linked together. Other genetic cousins with whom I had sent introductory messages never replied back at all.

One day in 2012, I came across one of my DNA matches who listed a surname that I was familiar with due to my years of Mississippi family research. The surname was Grantham. A branch of this family had married into the line of a slave owner whom my ancestors on my father's side of the family had been enslaved by, a slave owner by the name of Richard Eskridge, of Duck Hill, Mississippi (See the book *Akee Tree, A Descendant's Quest For His Slave Ancestors on the Eskridge Plantations*). So obviously I was quite excited to have this person's profile show up as one of my genetic cousins. An opportunity to meet another Eskridge relative. However, this person had not become related to me through the Eskridge family. According to our test results, we shared a common ancestor about <u>four generations back</u>, *PRIOR* to the time my paternal family came to the Eskridge plantation in Mississippi. This genetic cousin was Christine, and she was white. I sent Christine a message, asking if she cared to correspond, and the answer was yes. Christine sent the family history of her Grantham ancestor Richard Grantham, born in 1750 in North Carolina and later came to settle a plantation on the Neuse River near New Bern, North Carolina, an area notorious for enslaving Native American indigenous (See the Book *Three Brothers – 1626*, by the author). I studied her information with interest. Was she related to me because one of her white male ancestors had mated with one of my female black ancestors? Or, was it the other way around, one of my black male ancestors mating with one of her female white ancestors? But again, I was trying to fit her Grantham family history into my Eskridge family narrative, and therefore I was baffled, because it didn't fit into the narrative. And the reason it didn't fit was because Christine and I had become related through a different ancestor, at a time *prior* to when her Grantham branch had even married into the Eskridge line.

A year went by. Then two. Then two more. One weekend my wife and I were visiting her sister and family. We all went out to a nice Sunday brunch. Sitting around the serving table, my sister-in-law's daughter began reminiscing about her paternal grandmother's Southern cooking, since her grandmother was born and raised in the South. I asked the daughter what part of the South was her grandmother from. "Jackson, Mississippi," she replied. I then asked about her grandmother's maiden name. "Her maiden name was Grantham," she said. "What," I said in astonishment. I asked her to repeat everything again, making sure I understood what had just been said. Yes, it was true. I then explained to everyone at the table that my DNA match, Christine, also had ancestors named Grantham. "We might all be related," we joked. I was Black and they were White.

When later returning back home, I looked up the information that my sister-in-law's daughter gave me about her paternal grandmother. Turns out it wasn't a joke after all. My sister-in-law's children and I were related. One of their Grantham ancestors died in 1875 near Duck Hill, Mississippi. As it turns out, my sister-in-law's children's paternal line trace back to an individual named Edward Grantham IV. My DNA match, Christine, her family traces back to a Richard Grantham I. Apparently, Edward Grantham IV and Richard Grantham I *were brothers*, way back in the 1700's in Surry County, Virginia.

In 2016, I discovered there was a male Lipscomb cousin that appeared in my DNA results. This male was a sibling to one of the female Lipscomb cousins who were in my mother's family. In turn, they were matching two persons with the surname Collins.

I had never heard my mother or her mother (my Grandmother Lucy Shelton) mention anything about a family named Collins. Little did I realize that our connection to the Collins family would eventually lead me to an amazing discovery.

CHAPTER 6

An Amazing Clue

Two persons connected to a family named "Collins" showed up as new matches to my DNA results and to my maternal Lipscomb cousins.

The first of these two new matches I will refer to as Kersey. The second match I will call Collins.

Kersey appeared to be related to a particular branch of Black families named Collins from Georgia. There was a Charlie Collins, born around 1885, who was the son of Abe Collins and Easter Bell of Mt. Vernon, Georgia. Abe was born about 1853. In turn, Abe was the son of Andy and Caroline Collins. Andy Collins was born about 1826 and possibly from Liberty County, Georgia, located in the coastal basin of the Ogeechee River. However, I ran into a "brick wall" in trying to trace that branch of Andy Collins' family line.

On the other hand, thankfully with the help from genealogical records and cited sources posted in the public domain on the Internet, I was able to track the family line of the second new match, the one I call Collins. On the 1850 Federal Census for Ozark County, Missouri, I located Collins' fourth great-grandfather, Aaron Collins, born in 1773 in North Carolina, (other sources say Virginia), and the son of a David Collins and Thompsey Poston, married in Rowan County, North Carolina in 1772. This David Collins, in turn, is believed to be the son of a John Collins, born around 1734. John Collins was the son of a Thomas Collins, born 1710 in Louisa County, Virginia, and grandson of "Old Blind Collins" who was said to have married "a Saponi Indian." Tracking these "Sons" and "Fathers" is very important when engaging in Genealogy, as it helps in identifying the family you are researching, and avoids confusion with a different family. So now let me show you where this led me: Free People of Color.

There is documentation of a Thomas Collins in Louisa County, Virginia between 1745-1747. On May 28, 1745, the Louisa County Court "Ordered that William Hall, Samuel Collins, Thomas Collins, William Collins, Samuel Bunch, George Gibson, Benjamin Branham, Thomas Gibson, and William Donathan be summoned to appear at the next Court to answer the presentment of the Grand jury this day made against them for concealing tithables within twelve months past." Concealing tithables, what did that mean?

In 1658, when the Virginia assembly passed a law defining "What Persons are Tithable," the term meant a member of the productive labor force. The House of Burgesses session of September 1663 passed an act that every year masters were to give an exact account of tithables by June 10th to the legal authorities. A more complete law concerning tithables was passed by the House session in 1705. All free white males sixteen years of age and over, as well as all "Negro, mulatto, and Indian women sixteen years and over" were declared tithable. Each county court divided their county into precincts and annually appointed a justice for each district, who was to receive the list of tithables by June 10th.

In 1723, the House of Burgesses expanded the definition of a tithable to include all free Persons of Color above age sixteen and their wives. In an attempt to avoid paying levies, some masters removed their tithables from the county before the June 10th deadline.

In the House of Burgesses session of November 1738, an act was passed declaring any master engaging in the concealing of tithables would be fined. The act also stated that "mariners and seafaring persons," not being freeholders, were exempt from being listed as tithables. Who was considered a freeholder? Historically, the term meant a person who held ownership in land. The Colony of Virginia's voting law of 1736 defined a Freeholder as a white male 21 years of age who owned at least 100 acres of unimproved land or 25 acres of improved land with a house and plantation.

Apparently, these nine men were concealing their wives from being taxed as tithables. According to Virginia Law at that time, who was taxed and who was not? Free White women were not taxed. Slaves, Indians, Mulattos, and **Free Persons of Color – both men and women – were taxed.** So these nine men – either as a form of protest, a matter of honor and pride, or both – refused to allow their Free women of color to be subjected to a taxation, as if they were mere property. On June 25, 1745 the men pled not guilty in solidarity. Still, the case continued and a verdict was reached, but the decision was not recorded and thus unknown to this day.

So did this Thomas Collins have a free person of Color wife? Apparently so, according to this evidence. His wife may have been African, Indian, or mixed. Now my question became – was Thomas Collins white? In 1747, Thomas Collins sold 186 acres on the south side of the South Anna River. The land laid near the property of a Sam Bunch and a Thomas Gibson, the same names that appeared in the Court summons. Three years later in Granville County, North Carolina – on the border of Virginia – appears the 1750 tax list of Granville County, by the Flatt River. The familiar names Collins, Gibson, and Bunch all appear together:

Gideon Bunch 2 tithes

Thomas Collins Sr. 1 tithe

Samuel Collins 1 tithe

John Collins 1 tithe

Thomas Gibson

In 1753, Orange County was newly formed from Granville County. It included the Flatt River area. On the 1755 Tax List of Orange County, North Carolina appear those familiar names again:

Gedion Bunch 1 tithe (mulatto)

Thomas Collins 3 tithes (mulatto)

Samuel Collins 2 tithes (mulatto)

John Collins 1 tithe (mulatto)

Thomas Gibson 3 tithes (mulatto)

It seemed as though these families had a bond between them, a bond that seemed to have started in Virginia. These were mixed families, made up of perhaps African, European, and/or Native Indigenous.

My DNA Collins cousin had provided me with an amazing array of clues – but clues I still could not understand quite yet.

Returning to the census records, Collins' great-great-grandfather Leonard Collins was living in Howell County, Missouri in 1900. His family had made Howell County their home for over thirty years. My own mother was even born in Missouri, Pemiscott County, where Grandma Lucy raised the family. As I kept searching and digging for any evidence explaining how the Lipscombs became related to the Collins, I came across a 1910 newspaper account about a court case occurring in Howell County in 1891. It involved a lawsuit brought on by a family named Hall against the district school board for refusing the Hall children to attend a white school.

The Hall children were of very dark complexion, and so were barred from attending the all White school because the children were thought to be Black. However, the parents and other Hall relatives *claimed they were of Portuguese descent.* The ancestor of the Hall family in Howell County was Thomas Hall, who came to Missouri by 1850. Henderson Hall also migrated with him. *Their ancestry was said to have originated in Portugal.* Thomas Hall had even gone before a Tennessee court in 1835 to give a sworn affidavit that he was of Portuguese descent and therefore a free citizen.

The trial was moved to another Missouri county called Texas County. The suit went to court and much testimony was given. Thomas Hall's affidavit of 1835 was also introduced, the same papers he had filed in 1850 when he arrived in Missouri. The Halls won their suit. The testimony given satisfied the court that the ancestors of the Halls came from Portugal, and the family was now looked upon as Whites of Portuguese descent. Curious to find Thomas Hall and Henderson Hall in the census records, I finally found them on the 1850 Federal Census, Oregon County, Missouri. Both them and their families were all listed as "mulatto." On the 1860 Federal Census, Howell County, Henderson was listed as White. The newspaper stated that the early settlers looked upon Henderson Hall as a white man.

The facts I was discovering on this journey, amazing facts, were slowly turning into clues. My mind was awakened to the reminder that **Free People of Color** lived in America during slavery. I could not ignore researching the historical records about them.

Soon I began noticing certain patterns that would repeat themselves – becoming clues on this journey – the names Collins, Gibson, and Bunch seemed to appear together often, as well as more oral stories about Portuguese descent.

The next DNA cousin led me through another door towards my final destination.

CHAPTER 7
Another Cousin Unlocks Another Door

I sent a message to another name on my list of genetic matches. This person was said to be on my father's side of the family, and was the seventeenth match from the top out of over 200 on my second testing company's list. That meant we shared a fairly "high" percentage of DNA, compared to others who were lower on the list. His last name was Ivey.

There was no initial response to my message, which stated the *who, how,* and *why* of my purpose, along with a short bio about my ancestors. I waited a few months, and then decided to reach out again. This time I got a reply. Cousin Ivey asked if I was related to his paternal grandmother. All that I could honestly say was that I was hoping to try and find out. Our DNA showed we shared a common ancestor about four generations back. From his photo I knew he was Black, and he knew that of me based on mine. With the names of his father and grandparents I was supplied with, I began embarking on another new adventure, but ultimately the same journey.

What would I learn this time?

Cousin Ivey's maternal grandparents were Jessie and Anna Locker. His grandfather, Jessie Dwight Locker, was born in Cincinnati, Ohio in 1891. Jessie Dwight Locker became a lawyer and politician in Cincinnati, and was later appointed by President Eisenhower in

1953 as United States Ambassador to Liberia. He died in Office in Monrovia, Liberia on April 10, 1955.

Cousin Ivey's paternal grandparents were Earl and Goldie Ivey of Rains County, Texas. Earl Ivey's mother was Laura Ivey, born in 1867 and later married James Samuel. Laura's mother was Caroline Ivey, born around 1840. In 1880, Laura was living in Rains County along with her mother Caroline and Laura's five other siblings – Wallace, Alex, Anna, Polk, and Julia. Caroline was a widow by this time. Her husband's name remains unknown. It seemed obvious that she obtained her last name by marrying someone named Ivey. But then, there was also that slight chance she had given the census enumerator her maiden name. Caroline and her children were living in the household of a white family whom she worked for as a domestic.

Were there any other Black families with the surname Ivey in Rains County, Texas? There were two. The first was Henry Ivey, whose name was also spelled Ivy or Ivie, and was born about 1835. He had lived in Rains County for over 40 years, was both married and a widower three times, and was a wealthy man until his death in November 1921. A local newspaper noting his passing said this: "Uncle Henry Ivey, colored, died at his home on Lake Fork the 20th of November. He was possibly the most widely known colored man in this county, as he was brought here before the Civil War as a slave, and continued to live the balance of his life here after being granted his freedom… He was held in high esteem by both black and white and his word considered just as good as his note." Ten years after his death, another local newspaper paid tribute to him in 1931. The caption read "RICHEST CITIZEN OF COUNTY WAS A NEGRO." The article read: "In speaking of earlier days of his county, a well known minister who resides in Rains County said at one time the wealthiest citizen of that county was a Negro. His name was Henry Ivey. He inherited his fortune from his former owner. He established a settlement on a creek near where Emory, the county site, now stands."

Although still not certain if Henry Ivey was related to Caroline Ivey, two points stood out from both newspaper articles. First, Henry was brought to Texas as a slave *Before* the Civil War, and second, he inherited wealth from his former owner. I wondered if the former owner was perhaps Henry's father. Most slave owners I've researched did not usually bequeath a fortune to someone considered beneath them (a slave) in the social rank, unless some kind of personal and emotional connection existed.

What about Caroline's mother? She said her mother was from South Carolina. After 1880, Caroline disappears. I did not find another document about her. Nor did I find her children after 1880, except for Laura, now married to James Samuel from Tennessee, and her older brother Alex.

Still not able to make a connection between Caroline Ivey and Henry Ivey, I now turned my attention to Cousin Ivey's paternal grandmother, Goldie Ivey, to locate her maiden name and family. *The marriage records revealed* **the maiden name of Collins**. That was quite a surprise. There was the name Collins again. I began to wonder if Goldie Ivey's Collins' ancestors pointed to my family line. Goldie's parents were Fletcher and Ollie Collins, and her grandparents Peter and Francis Collins, both from Alabama and Georgia, respectively. Peter and Francis Collins, when their son Fletcher was a child, were for a time living in Cass County, Texas by 1880, right on the border of Louisiana near Shreveport. Did Goldie Ivey's Collins ancestors come out of Creole Louisiana? Then all of a sudden, I noticed something major.

In 1910, living right next door to Goldie Collins and her grand-parents, the Hills, was Henry Ivey. Not only that, but counting six houses down was Laura Ivey, her daughter, and Laura's husband. This was a huge discovery. Not only did this perhaps explain how Cousin Ivey's grandparents eventually met each other, but also, this was so far the best evidence I had found placing Henry Ivey and Caroline Ivey's daughter Laura that close together – within six houses – suggesting they were indeed related.

So who was the slave owner who "brought [Henry] here before the Civil War as a slave" and "inherited his fortune from his former owner"?

How did Henry Ivey receive his freedom from slavery? The ar-ticle about his life said Henry continued to live the balance of his life in Rains County "after being granted his freedom." Did a slave owner grant his freedom? The 1850 and 1860 Federal Population Schedules for the State of Texas listed no such Henry Ivey as a free man, or any other variation spelling of the surname. On the other hand, the 1850 Slave Schedules for Texas showed Micajah "Cage Ivy" with a twelve-year-old male slave in Panola County, and in 1860 with a twenty-one year old male slave in Hunt County. That might have been Henry.

So who were the Iveys of South Carolina? What I learned had me awakened again. You just couldn't make this up.

In August 1809 in Marion District, South Carolina, a man named Thomas Hagans was assessed a required tax. Only "Free Negroes, Mulattos, and Mestizos" were required to pay this annual poll tax. Thomas Hagans refused to pay the tax, claiming he was white. *Thomas Hagans' defense was that his grandfather "Thomas Ivey was Portuguese."* Thomas Hagans brought his dispute to court and resulted in a trial. Two men who knew the grandfather Thomas Ivey were called to testify. One of the men, a neighbor of Ivey's son

Thomas Ivey Jr., stated that Thomas Ivey was once a resident of Bladen County, North Carolina but moved to South Carolina sometime in the 1760's. The other man testified that Thomas Ivey and his wife had lived in Marion District for several years. Both men stated that Thomas Ivey was of "Portuguese descent, that his complexion was swarthy, his hair black and straight...his wife was a free white woman, very clear complexion." Based on the testimony, the court's ruling was that Thomas Hagan was not subject to the tax because he was not black, but was of Portuguese descent.

So just like the trial in Howell County, Missouri in 1891, here was another court case eighty years earlier, about families having to testify about their dark skin, and that they were Portuguese.

There was also yet another similar trial. In Chattanooga, Tennessee, Jerome Simmerman and Jemima Bolton were married in the 1850's. In 1858, Jemima died during childbirth of their daughter. The child, Martha Bolton, was eventually sent to Illinois to live with her aunt. Sixteen years later by 1874, Jerome Simmerman could no longer handle his financial estate due to his mental state of mind. The rightful heir to inherit the estate was his daughter Martha Bolton. But Jerome's relatives claimed that his deceased wife Jemima was "colored" and therefore Martha could not be a legal heir because the marriage was forbidden under State law. A lawsuit was filed and the case went to court. Martha's lawyer, Lewis Shepherd, contended that Martha's mother Jemima Bolton was not "colored" because her grandfather, Spencer Bolton, was Portuguese. Evidence was presented. Drury Dobbins Scruggs, who knew the grandfather Spencer Bolton when he lived in South Carolina, gave testimony:

Q. State whether or not you were acquainted with a man named Spencer Bolton in Spartanburg District South Carolina?

A. I knew him.

Q. State to what race of people Bolton belonged, and state fully all the facts in connection with your acquaintance with him and his family?

A. He belonged to the Spanish race of people I think. I am positive that it was either Spanish or Portuguese. I was Tax Collector in the District at one time and amongst other things I was required to levy a per capita tax on all Negroes and I recollect distinctly that it was not levied by me upon him. He, Bolton was a dark skinned man with very straight hair and long nosed, thin visaged man. At the time referred to when I was tax collector, some parties reported to me that Bolton was of mixed blood. Thereupon I proceeded to investigate the matter by calling in three citizens living in his neighborhood, among whom were a Mr. Young, Mr. Miles, and other to assist me in deciding the question; the decision was in favor of Bolton, to the effect he had no Negro blood in him. About the same time my attention was also called in an official capacity to a Mr. Dempsey who claimed to be a Portuguese, and the decision in his case was that he was of mixed blood, but I gave him the right of appeal but he left the country. Bolton and Dempsey were not in any way connected."

The lawyer, in his argument that Martha Bolton was not of African descent, said that she was a "Melungeon." Years later the lawyer, now Judge Lewis Shepherd explained this in his memoirs:

> "These people belonged to a peculiar race, which settled in East Tennessee at an early day…known as Melungeons…a colony of these Moors crossed the Atlantic before the Revolutionary War and settled on the coast of South Carolina. They multiplied rapidly and by this industry and energy they accumulated considerable property. The South Carolina people, however, would not receive them on terms of equality. They refused to recognize them specially and would not allow the children to go to school with them."

I had never heard of the word "Melungeon" until one day, years ago inside a local genealogy library, when one of the library's organizers, mentioned that I should investigate if I might be Melungeon. I thanked him for the suggestion, but it went over my head. Being that I was so involved in researching other leads about family history at the time, I never did investigate his suggestion. Now I wanted to learn more.

Isaiah Ivy, born around 1775 near the North and South Carolina border, left Marion District, South Carolina and headed to Mississippi, and then later bringing his wife, eight sons, and two daughters to Texas, where he died in 1844. At least one of his sons, Micajah "Cage" Ivy, brought his family and slaves to Hunt County, Texas. Another son, or relative of Isaiah Ivy, Magirt Ivy, also settled nearby with his family. Both were born in South Carolina, Magirt in 1799, and Micajah "Cage" in 1805. By 1860, Magirt had died, and Micajah the same by 1866. Edie Ivy, a former female enslaved person, was tending to Magirt's widow Rosanna Ivy of Hunt County in 1870.

What would I find out about Isaiah Ivy's ancestors? Were they free people of color?

Isaiah Ivy was the son of James Ivey and Mourning Driggers of Marlboro District. James and Mourning Ivey had six sons – James, Joseph, Curtis, Micajah, Magirt, and Isaiah, as mentioned.

The father James Ivey was born sometime in the 1740's. He died in Marlboro County, South Carolina in 1820 and left a last will bequeathing his last effects and nine slaves. What is said next is particularly important in helping to identify him among the court records. Between 1769 and 1772, James Ivey was residing in Bladen County, North Carolina, based on his Grantor land deed of 1769, and his name appearing on the Bladen tax lists along with a *Joseph Ivey*, Thomas Ivey, and a *Gideon Grant*. (Bladen County, NC is right on the Carolina border of Marion District, SC). James Ivey was also at one time living in Richmond County, North Carolina. This is based on a land claim there in 1783 by a landholder, who mentions land improvements "made by James Ivey and *Boson Cheves*. (Richmond County, NC is right on the Carolina border of Marlboro District, SC and Marlboro District borders Marion District, SC). By 1790, James Ivey and Joseph Ivey had already crossed the border into South Carolina, James having moved to the area of present Marion County, and Joseph to the area of present Marlboro County. James eventually settled in Marlboro. Both men were later laid to rest there, James in 1820, and Joseph in 1857. With all that being said now comes the part that completely shook me, consisting of two documents.

First, on the 1790 South Carolina census, Joseph Ivey is listed as "mulatto" with 3 males over 16 and 3 females, all listed as "**other** free persons." The second document, dated December 13, 1773, was a message from the North Carolina Governor to the State Assembly with a letter enclosed from a justice of Bladen County entitled "A list of the mob raitously assembled together in Bladen County October 13th 1773." At the bottom of the letter is written: **"The above list of rogues is all free negroes and mulattus living upon the King's land."** The letter contained the names of eighteen "free negroes and mulattoes who infest that county and annoy its inhabitants." The free men of color trespassing on the King's Land were, (in order as originally spelled) as follows:

"**Captain James Ivey**
Joseph Ivey
Ephraim Sweat
William Chavours Clark commonly called **Boson Chevers**
Richd. Groom
Bengman [Benjamin?] Deel also possibly Dees
Willm. Sweat
George Sweat
Benjamin Sweat
Willm Groom Senr
Willm, Groom Junr.
Gideon Grant
Thos. Groom
James Pace
Isaac Vaun
--- Stapleton
Edward Lockelear
Ticely Lockalear

Harbourers of the rogues as follows:

Major Lockalear
Richer Groom
Ester Cairsey

The above list of rogues is **all free negroes and mulattus** living upon the King's land"

There was no question these North Carolina men, James Ivey and Joseph Ivey, were the same two who later settled in Marlboro County, South Carolina. The names of two men, Boson Chevers and Gideon Grant, had been listed earlier with James Ivey's name from the Bladen tax lists and a land deed. The fact that James Ivey was called "Captain" may have indicated that he was the leader of this group. Joseph Ivey may have been James' brother or a relative, the "mulatto" Joseph Ivey who died in 1857. The 1850 Marlboro County Census indicated that he had been born about 1757.

Were James and Joseph Ivey the ancestors of my genetic match Cousin Ivey? They were free Blacks, and a trail from them went directly to the area of Rains County, Texas.

But that still didn't answer my other question: why were so many going to court over Race and claiming Portuguese descent? The final DNA cousins would eventually lead me to an astonishing answer of historical proportions.

CHAPTER 8

Cousins Connected to 1619

Still determined to trace my mother's family through my Grandma Lucy Lipscomb Shelton, I went back to the drawing board – the DNA results that I shared with my Lipscomb cousins. I was also still just as much determined to traverse Grandmother Marcella Barnett's ancestors too, if they could be found. One day in May 2016 came an incredible turning point. I was reviewing notes about Charles Barnett of Albemarle, Virginia, the Free Person of Color, who was a bondsman on January 3, 1791 to the marriage of Richard Brock and Mary Goin. Mary was the daughter of a Benjamin Goin, also a free person of Color. His family last name was sometimes spelled Goings. Then, as I was comparing Lipscomb DNA matches to mine for more possible new clues, I found one – we both had matches to persons named *Goins* and *Goings*. This surname has several variation spellings.

And – this surname showed up on my father's side of the family as well.

I sent four emails to these new matches, and they all replied back. Two of them said that their family origins started in Virginia, and that both of their family's migration patterns were "Virginia-Ohio-Indiana." One of them continued to Iowa.

One of them had a direct ancestor to Albemarle County, Virginia. His ancestor's name was Wilson Middlebrook Goins, born in 1795. His descendants migrated to Athens County, Ohio. While searching high and low for genealogical information about him, I ended up coming across several articles about persons who claimed they had descended from the first Africans who came to Virginia in 1619.

I was numb. Could this really be true? Are there families today in America who descend from the first Africans brought to the shores of Virginia in 1619? I remember being taught about that event in 7th grade in the early 1970's. "Yeah, they were indentured servants," my brother said, as we recalled those school sessions. I also came across an article written by research author Tim Hashaw, and how he had discovered he was a descendant of the first Africans while tracing his family line (Sources, Chapter 8). Reading his article had me totally stunned and mesmerized – that there are descendants who can prove that they are genetically related to those first Africans of Virginia, North America. I felt jubilation. I felt the joy of an archaeologist when finding a discovery.

My DNA cousins – Grantham, Collins, Ivey, and now Goins – each of them had caused me to arrive back in the classroom, as it were, and experience that moment we all have had when something you've learned for the first time changes your life in some small or large way – just as it did me in 7th grade when I first learned of Black indentured servants and Black cowboys who were not slaves.

One of the first Africans in 1619, whose name appeared in a court record dated March 31, 1641, was "John Geaween", an indentured servant for a planter named William Evans in the Colony of Virginia:

> "Whereas it appeareth to this court that John Geaween being a negro servant unto William Evans was permitted by his said master to keep hogs and make the best benefit

thereof to himself provided that the said Evans might have half the increase, which was accordingly returned unto him by the said negro and the other half reserved for his own benefit: And whereas the said negro having a young child of a negro woman belonging to Lieut. Robert Sheppard which he desired should be made a Christian and be brought up in the fear of God and in the knowledge of religion taught and exercised in the church of England, by reason whereof he the said negro did for his said child purchase its freedom of Lieut. Robert Sheppard with the good liking and consent of Tho: Gooman's overseer, as by the deposition of the said Sheppard and Evans appeareth, the court hath therefore ordered that the child shall be free from the said Evans or his assigns and to be and remain at the disposing and education of the said Geaween and the child's god father, who undertaketh to see it brought up in the Christian religion as aforesaid."

This is the first recording of a "John Geaween" in the Virginia Colony. In time, the name would be anglized to "Gowen" and then finally to "Goins". The African was not a slave for life. He was an indentured servant, and indentured out for a definite time period. On average, an indenture could last from 4 to 10 years for most servants, regardless of race, in the early history of the Colony of Virginia. In the 17th century, most servants arriving in Virginia had signed voluntary Indenture contracts, which were legal documents containing the terms of agreement for a servant's labor. But there were also many servants who performed involuntary Indentures, forced servitude. Agents who worked for ship captains or merchants recruited most servants in England. Upon arrival into Virginia, the plantation owners, called planters, would bargain with the ship captains or their agents to purchase the Indenture servant and their contract.

The average term of indenture for those entering voluntarily was four years for servants twenty years of age or over. Servants coming to the colonies without indentures were bound according to the custom of the country. Servants between sixteen and twenty could be bound from six to eight years. Whereas, those under sixteen often served until they reached the age of twenty-one. In some cases, the indenture time was extended. When the terms of Indenture had been met, the servant was then set free. This included African servants as well. The social rank in early Virginia life was the same as in England. At the top of the social level were the Gentlemen. The Planters followed them. Next came the Yeomen, followed by the servant. Thus, in England and in early Virginia, it was a person's social status that defined their rank in society, not the color of skin. In fact, during the early beginnings of the Virginian colony, England had not yet involved itself in the Atlantic Slave Trade. For a time, there was no such thing as African slaves in England or Virginia.

John Geaween the African had mated with a Black woman during his servitude to William Evans. The woman, a servant to Evans neighbor, Lieutenant Robert Sheppard, gave birth to a child. John Geaween in time purchased his young child's freedom from Lieutenant Sheppard, and the court ordered that the child be set free. We know nothing about Geaween's parentage or his age. He was likely born in Africa. However, if we were to assume that he was *at least* 15 or 16 years of age in order to father a child, then subtracting that from the year of the court order, would bring Geaween to a birth year of 1625, assuming he was only a teen. But the African seemed older than that. It appeared he possessed the maturity of an adult, concerned with the future welfare of his child by saving his earnings to purchase the child's freedom. Geaween's move to approach the court reflected his intelligence to use the legal system to his benefit. Perhaps he saw or sensed something changing in the Virginia world around him in regards to the free status of he and his African countrymen in the colony. Perhaps he feared that his child might inherit the status of his mother. Little did he know that by the year 1660, the laws would change drastically for Africans in the colony, such as the law "All children born in this country shall be held bond or free only according to the condition of the mother." No doubt he had heard, perhaps even seen, what had occurred at the neighboring plantation of Lieutenant Sheppard, when one of his female servants had been whipped:

> "*Whereas Robert Sweat* hath begotten with child a negro woman servant belonging unto Lieutenant *Sheppard, the court hath therefore ordered* that the said negro woman shall be whipt at the whipping post and the said *Sweat* shall tomorrow in the forenoon do public penance for his offence at *James city* church in the time of devine service according to the laws of *England* in that case provided." 17 October 1640

Some say the woman servant was the very mother of Geaween's child whose freedom he was obtaining thru the court. Whether or not that was true, it clearly showed that the laws in the colony were changing. Previous to this, it was not unlawful for a white man and a black woman to bear a child if in the bounds of matrimony. But now, it was against the law to bear a mulatto child. And should a child be born from a secret marriage or out of wedlock during the mother's term of indenture, the child would be indentured to the parish until the age of twenty-one if male and age eighteen if female. One can only wonder as to what prompted Geaween to document his child's freedom before the court, which also had ordered that his child be free from any claim of William Evans and his heirs too.

Clearly, Geaween was among the first generation Africans in Virginia. Based on my research, there was a good chance Geaween may have been born around 1610 in Africa. Upon arriving in Virginia in 1619 – or even by 1625 – he would have been under age sixteen and required to be indentured until the age of twenty-one, "according to the custom of the country." For example, if he had arrived under age in 1619 at age nine, or 1620 by age ten, he would have reached the age of twenty-one by the year 1631. Of course, the adjudging of Geaween's age when he arrived into the colony may have occurred by master William Evans, unless Evans was somehow able to ascertain Geaween's correct age by means of an interpreter or some other way. And who was to say whether Geaween "volunteered" to serve another Indenture for his master William Evans after he turned twenty-one? According to the court document in 1641, Geaween and Evans appeared to have been on good terms, as Evans allowed Geaween to reclaim his child. He was also "permitted by his master to keep hogs and make the best benefit thereof to himself provided that the said Evans might have half the increase." Geaween was no doubt engaging in something in order to acquire earnings for the purchase of his child, whether that was from selling some of his hogs or by some other means of endeavor, and could have indentured himself to buy himself more time to build his savings. Additionally, Geaween, Evans, and Lieutenant Sheppard may also have been adjudging the age of Geaween's child in 1641 before the courts. If true, that might have indicated that the child was under the age of twelve, the age when "Negro children" were judged to be tithables.

Many researchers of John Geaween's family line say his child's name was Mihil. There is a court document involving a "Negro" servant named "Mihil Gowen" in York County, Virginia. York County was formed in 1643. Part of that county's area during 1619 was called James City. That was the city where many of the Africans, in 1619 and in several years afterward, were assigned to live. During his four years of service, Mihil mated with a Black woman named Prosta (some say Prossa), and a male child was born named William in 1655. Two years later, in 1657, Anne Amy Barnhouse, acting on behalf of her brother Christopher Stafford, now deceased, discharged Mihil from further service, and also returned his son William. She makes two declarations on record about Mihil and William:

> "Bee it known unto all Christian people that whereas Mihill Gowen Negro of late servant to my Brother Xopher Stafford deced by his last will & Testament bearing Date the 18 of Jan 1654 had his freedom given unto him after the expiration of 4 yeares service unto my uncle Robert Stafford Therefore know all whom it may concern that I Anne Barnehouse for divers good couses mee hereunto moving doe absolutely quitt & discharge the sd Mihill Gowen from any service & for ever sett him free from any claim of service either by mee or any one my behalf as any part or parcell of my Estate that my be claimed by mee the said Amy Barnhouse my heyres Exers Admrs or Assignes as witness my hand this 25 Oct 1657 Amy (AB) Barnhouse"

> "Bee it knowne unto all Xcian people that I Ame Barnehouse of Martins hundred widdow for divers good causes & consideracons mee hereunto moving hath given unto Mihill Gowen Negro hee being att this time servant unto Robert Stafford a Male child borne the 25 Aug 1655 of the body of

my Negro Prosta being baptised by Mr. Edward Johnson 2 Sept 1655 & named William & I the said Amy Barnhouse doth bind my selfe my heyres Exer Admr & Ass never to trouble or molest the said Mihill Gowin or his sone William or demand any service of the said Mihill or his said sone William In witness whereof I have caused this to be made & done I hereunto sett my hand & Seale this present 16 Sept 1655 Amy (AB) Barnhouse."

Mihil very likely was the son of Geaween, or closely related, since Amy Barnhouse identified Mihil with the surname "Gowen". Based on further calculations and on the laws at that time, Mihil may have been born about 1632. If we study the court documents of Amy Barnhouse, she stated that Mihil "being *at this time* servant unto Robert Stafford." That "time" would have been September 1655, the date of her statement. Then two years later we read: "Be it known…*had* his freedom given unto him *after* the expiration of 4 years service unto my uncle Robert Stafford." This meant that as of the date of that statement, October 1657, Mihil *had* been given his freedom, BECAUSE it was *after* the expiration of the 4 years of service. Between 1655 and 1656, the 4-year Indenture had not yet been completed. But by October 1657, Amy Barnhouse now had the reason and the basis for announcing her declaration. This meant that the 4-year Indenture began around September 1653! Christopher Stafford was still alive then as well, who entered the terms of Mihil's contract into his last will & testament on January 18, 1654. The reason that Christopher Stafford already knew Mihil was because the under aged African had been Indentured earlier to him until Mihil reach twenty-one. And if we count 21 years backwards from 1653 we arrive at the year Mihil was possibly born.

Mihil Gowen later received a land grant for 37 acres on February 8, 1668 in James City County to live out his days as a free man. Sometime between 1708 and 1717, Mihil Gowen was deceased, and his land lay as unclaimed property. Nothing more is known about his son William, nor of William's mother Prosta. However, there was another African descended male in James City, around the same time that Mihil Gowen was living on his land, who went by the last name of Gowen. His name was Phillip Gowen. Some researchers say Mihil Gowen later married a Scotch-Irish woman and they had four sons together.

On July 16, 1674, Phillip Gowen filed a petition for his freedom in James City County against a Charles Lucas, stating that he had been the servant of Mrs. Amy Beazley, deceased, of James City County (this was Amy Barnhouse, who earlier released Mihil Gowen from her service; Amy had since remarried), who in her last will & testament dated April 9, 1664, had appointed Phillip to serve her cousin Humphrey Stafford for a term of eight years and then be given his freedom, along with being paid three barrels of corn and a suit of clothes. But, soon after Amy Beazley departed this life, Humphrey Stafford sold the remainder of Phillip's term to Charles Lucas, who, instead of releasing Phillip after his eight-year term of service, tricked Phillip into signing an indenture for twenty years in Warwick County, Virginia. Warwick County, now extant, was located on the northern bank of the James River between Hampton Roads and Jamestown. Phillip also wrote to the Governor Sir William Berkeley:

> The petition of Phillip Gowen a Negro, In all humility Sheweth: That your petitioner being a servant: to Mrs. Amye Beazlye late of James City County Widow decd. the said Mrs. Beazlye made her last will & testament in writ-

ting under her hand & seal, bearing date the 9th day of Aprill An Dom. 1664: and amongst other things, did order, will, & appoint, that yor. petr. by the then name of Negro Boy Phillip, should serve her Cousin Mr: Humphrey Stafford, the term of Eight years then next ensuing, and then should enioy his freedom & be paid three barrells of Corn & a suit of Clothes, As by the said will appears, Soon after the making of which will, the said Mrs. Beazlye departed this life, and your petr. did continue & abide with the said Mr. Stafford (with whom he was orderd by the said will to live) some years, and then the said Mr. Stafford sold the remainder of your. petrr. time, to one Mr. Charles Lucas, with whom your petr also continued, doing true & faithful Service, but the said Mr: Lucas coveting yr petrs.

Service longer then of right it was due, did not at the expiration of the said Eight years, discharge your petr. from his service, but compelled him to serve three years longer than the time set by the said Mrs: Beazleys will, and then not being willing yr. petr. should enioy his freedom, did contrary to all honesty & good conscience, with threats & a high hand, in the time of your. petrs. Service with him, and by his confedracy with some persons, compel your. petr. to set his hand to a writing, which the said Mr. Lucas now saith, is an Indenture for twenty years, and forced your. petr. to acknowledge the same in the County court of Warwick.

Now for that may it please your. honors: your. petr. was at the time of the making this said forced writing, in the service of the said Mr. Lucas and never discharged from the same, the said Mr: Lucas alwaies uniustly pretending that your. petr. was to serve him three years longer, by an order of Court is untrue, which pretenses of the said

Mr. Lucas will appear to your. honors. by t[he] testimony of persons of good credit: Your: Petr. therefore most humbly prayeth your. honors. to order that the said writing so forced from him be made void; and that the said Mr. Luca[s] make him satisfaction for the said three years service above his tim[e] and pay him Corn & Clothes with costs of Suit: And your. petr. (as in duty bound) shall ever pray &c.

The James City Court ruled:

"It is ordered that the said Phill Gowen be free from ye said Mr. Lucas his Service and that the Indenture Acknowledg'd in Warwick County be Invalid and that ye Said Mr. Lucas pay unto ye Gowen three Barrells of Corn at the Crop According to ye Will of Mrs Amye Beazlye decd with costs…"

So, besides Mihil Gowen and his son William serving Amy Stafford Barnhouse Beazley's family the Staffords, we now learn that Phillip Gowen was also serving her family during the same time period, just before the date of her signed will in 1664. Was Phillip another son of Mihil Gowen? Why did Phillip take the last name Gowen and not some other surname? It seems very likely, therefore, that Phillip was another son of Mihil Gowen, or closely related. Whether Mihil went on to have had other children, the record does not say. Other persons named "Goins" and "Goen" began to show up in Westmoreland and Stafford County, Virginia. On September 29, 1697, "Thomas Goen Confesses judgment" to a Charles Lucas in the amount of 1, 250 pounds of tobacco in Westmoreland County (not the same Charles Lucas which Phillip Gowen was Indentured to). In 1710, Thomas Goins, John Goins, William Goins, and James Goins received 1215 acres in Stafford County (formed from Westmoreland in 1664). No indication is made as to the Race of these four persons if they were not white. However, during a Court land dispute some fifty-seven years later involving one of the Goins' neighbors, Major Robert Alexander, a witness named Charles Griffith related that in a conversation, Major Alexander had said about the "Goings", that "he had a great mind to turn the Molatto rascals off his land." The Goins were involved in horseracing contests at the time. The witness Griffith went on to give context to Major Alexander's conversation, "he was at a race in the same year when the Goings were (who then had running horses) and that the old people were talking about the Goings taking up Alexanders land and selling it to Thomas and Todd…"

"*Molatto* rascals off his land." That was an indication about the race of that group of Goins who had moved out to Stafford County.

It is unknown whether John Geaween's child, or Mihil's son William, or Phillip Gowen, or the group in Stafford County, had begot children. It is also unclear if John Geaween or Mihil had begot any more children. And, who were their wives? However, what is clear is that other families with their surname continued to spring up and migrate. It is also clear that other Africans landed in Virginia the year after 1619, and in the years after that. Where in Africa did they come from, and what became their story living in America?

CHAPTER 9

"Twenty & Odd Negroes"

It was towards the end of the month, on one peculiar day in August 1619, when the widowed husband of Pocahontas, John Rolfe, saw a ship approaching the Virginia Colony. The ship entered the harbor and dropped anchor. Rolfe saw that the name of the vessel was *White Lion*. He later wrote what occurred:

> "About the latter end of August, a Dutch man of Warr of the burden of 160 tons arrived at Point Comfort, the Comandor's name was Capt. Jope, his Pilot for the West Indies one Mr. Marmaduke an Englishman...He brought not anything but 20 and odd Negroes, which the Governor and Cape Merchant bought for victualle [whereof he was in great need as he pretended] at the best and easiest rate they could."

So, the twenty-some "Negroes" were "acceptable" to being brought into the colony. Their "Ellis Island" entry started out as an exchange for food. They looked like promising workers that could be used for useful labor, just like the rest of the Indentured servants who had been brought here. Once the Africans proved themselves industrious and productive over time, then no doubt they too, would be given the same opportunity as everyone else desired – to be free, to work, to own land, to prosper, and to become a contributing neighbor to this community. The Africans had already possessed that type of ideal living back home before the wars came to their villages.

Cape Merchant Abraham Peirsey and the Colony Governor, Sir George Yeardley, completed the deal with the ship captain for the Africans and then took them to their plantations. Sir George Yeardley, born in Surrey in 1587 and who survived for 10 months a ship wreak in Bermuda in 1609, owned a tobacco plantation upriver on the south side of the James River. The plantation was named Flowerdew Hundred. The name Flowerdew was also the maiden name of his wife, Lady Temperance. As for Abraham Peirsey, he was a merchant trader who sold goods to the colonists. How many of the twenty or so Africans Yeardley and Peirsey each took are unknown. About three or four days later, the other pirate ship, *Treasurer*, anchored at Point Comfort, and bringing 25 to 29 enslaved captives that were sold from Angola and now seized from the Spanish ship *Bautista* bound for Vera Cruz. As soon as Governor Yeardley was informed of this second ship's arrival, dispatched secretary John Rolfe, Mr. Ewens, and Lieutenant William Peirce to meet him at the ship.

How this second group of 25 or more were divided is also not known, however tobacco planter William Peirce did take a woman among this group whose name was "Angelo." Not all of this number may have been left in Virginia, as it had been said that the ship captain of *Treasurer* was planning to trade off some of his kidnapped group in Bermuda.

Although there was an obvious language barrier at the time some from the group climbed out of both ships and stood on soil before the Virginian men, it was no doubt noted, either right then or later when taken to Jamestown, that some of the Africans had European names, and spoke some words that would be understood by a Spanish interpreter. Spain and Portugal had hundreds of words with similar pronunciation and identical meaning. That also went for Biblical and religious words. Many in Ndongo and Kongo had been baptized and practicing Portuguese Catholicism, so this fact would also have become known to the colonists. Even if their religious conversions in Ndongo and Kongo may have been more for social or political reasons, the Angolans' knowledge of Christendom would have pulled considerable weight among the Virginian colonists because, at that time in England and in Virginia, social rank in society was determined, not by Race, but by Class and Religion, "Christian" or "Heathen." But in time, sadly, that social viewpoint would eventually change.

By March 1620, a census conducted by the Virginia colonists revealed there were 32 Africans in the colony that year, 15 males and 17 females. This number may reflect the actual number of Angolans who were brought roughly six months earlier in late August 1619. Or, the number was higher and some had been transported elsewhere, or perhaps died. Disease was already a constant threat in the colony. Some of the Africans might also have been exposed to sickness prior to their arrival. Malnutrition and famine had also been a problem in the Virginia colony in prior years. There was also the threat of being attacked by local native Indians whose lands the colonists were occupying. In early 1619, Lieutenant William Peirce and Sir George Yeardley had made a treaty with the Chickahominy Indians. But on March 22, 1622, there was an attack on the colony by the Powhatan Indians. One African named Antonio, who had been brought to the colony in 1621, was working on the Edward Bennett plantation when the attack reached there. The staged uprising killed about 347 colonists along the James River plantations, including 52 at Bennett's plantation. Antonio was one of four men who managed to survive the attack. At the Flowerdew Hundred Plantation, owned by Sir George Yeardley, six persons were killed.

According to the 1624 census, 11 Africans were living at the Flowerdew Hundred plantation. Only four names are known – Anthony, William, John, and another Anthony. The woman Angelo who came in 1619 was listed as living at Lieutenant Peirce's household. Four Africans lived at the puritan Edward Bennett's plantation – Peter, Frances, Margaret, and Antonio. The next year, the 1625 muster showed 3 males and 5 females living at Yeardley's residence at Jamestown, and four men, two women, and a child living at Flowerdew Hundred. On September 19, 1625, the General Court awarded temporary custody of an African man named Brass (or Brase) to Yeardley's wife, Lady Temperance Yeardley. The court also ordered to pay forty pounds of good tobacco per month for his labor as long as Brass remained under her service, and for Captain Nathaniel Bass to provide clothing to him. Brass had come to Virginia on a ship called *Portugal* with a Captain Jones, who later sold Brass to Nathaniel Bass, whose plantation was next to the Edward Bennett plantation. After the court gave Lady Temperance temporary custody of Brass, two weeks later he was transferred to the custody of the new Virginia colony's governor, Sir Francis Wyatt, and the sale to Captain Nathaniel Bass was voided. Also on the 1625 muster census was an African named John Pedro, assigned to Francis West in Elizabeth City, and an African couple named Anthony and Isabella, living at the residence of Captain William Tucker in Elizabeth City. Anthony and Isabella also had a male infant named William. The child was not listed on the 1624 census, which indicated the infant was born in 1625, or in 1624 after the census was taken.

Life went on for the remaining Ndongo and Congolize who arrived in Virginia from 1619 to 1628. Those Africans who had finished out their Indented servitude were pronounced free, and now able to acquire land and become property owners. Free Black women were not required to be tithed, but were kept exempt right along with the English women. Free Black men who owned land were not legally barred from buying the contracts of other indentured servants – Englishmen, Africans, or Indians – in order to provide labor for their lands, as long as the rules remained fair and equitable for all parties. Free Africans were not barred from marrying any woman who was free to marry in the colony, regardless of race. Their children were born free, whether black, mulatto, or mestizo, and were allowed to be baptized and be recognized as "Christian." They also began calling one another "Malunga," to remember who they were.

While at the same time Queen Nzinga of Ndongo was fighting another Portuguese assault on her kingdom, a slave ship named *Fortune* docked at the port of Virginia in 1628 from Angola, carrying 128 enslaved prisoners. Soon, they were unloaded and dispersed out to the several tobacco plantations along the James River and other county masters, to begin their time as Indentured servants. No doubt many of them were shocked but perhaps uplifted in spirit to be met by a community from their language-speaking homelands already here.

The Kongo community in the colony continued to grow, as more family alliances emerged, marriages took place and children grew up, ready to take their place in the world, receiving training in various occupation skills from their parents, grandparents, and others. But these freedoms they were enjoying would soon begin to be snatched away bit by bit. One day in 1639, a law was passed in the colony that Blacks could no longer possess firearms:

"ALL persons except negroes to be provided with arms and ammunition or be fined at pleasure of the Governor and Council"

That was surprising. Up until then, the statute since 1619 required everyone to attend church on the Sabbath and added:

"and all such as bear arms shall bring their pieces, swords, powder and shot."

In fact, a person would be fined if failing to do so. The threat of Indian attack at that time was real. No one was to go out in the fields unarmed. Even a sentry was to be standing guard nearby. The 1619 statute was reissued again in 1632:

"All men that are fitting to bear arms, shall bring their pieces to the church…"

Was this new edict an indication that the Africans in the colony were no longer trusted? This new law did not just come overnight. A thought process had been put into it over an unknown length of time by the framers. But if it was based upon some misunderstanding trust issue due to some isolated incidents from a few persons, it would be no reason to penalize the entire African community. That would be the same as penalizing the entire colony based on the conduct of a few unlawful English servants. However, it was no secret that since 1619, the Africans were sometimes treated slightly different than the rest in the minds of some in the community, and even among some in the House of Burgesses. But, as a whole, tolerance and industriousness up to now had been the colony's two best virtues. The young colony was still a growing experiment in meshing together different cultures – English, African, and Native Indian. Which would eventually win out – equity toward all, or pride, power, and intolerance? The answer would be made clear soon. Two runaway cases came before the Courts in July of 1640:

"Whereas Hugh Gwyn hath by order from this Board brought back from Maryland three servants formerly run away from the said Gwyn, the court doth therefore order that the said three servants shall receive the punishment of whipping and to have thirty stripes apiece one called Victor, a [D]utchman, the other a Scotchman called James Gregory, shall first serve out their times with their master according to their Indentures and one whole year apiece after the time of their service is Expired…the third being a Negro named John Punch shall serve his said master and his assigns for the time of his natural Life here or elsewhere" 9th July 1640

"Whereas complaint has been made to this Board by Capt Wm Pierce Esqr that six of his servants and a negro of Mr Reginolds has plotted to run away unto the Dutch plantation from their said masters and did assay to put the same in Execution upon Saturday night being the 18th day July 1640 as appeared to the Board by Examinations of Andrew Noxe, Richd Hill, Richd Cookeson and John Williams and likewise by confession of Christopher Miller, Peter Wilcocke, and Emanuel the foresaid Negro who had at the fore said time, taken the skiff of the said Capt Wm Pierce their master, and corn powder and shot guns, to accomplish their said purposes, which said p[er]sons sailed down in the said skiff to Elizabeth river where they were taken and brought back again, the Court taking the same into consideration, as a dangerous p[re]cident for the future time did order that Christopher Miller a Dutchman should receive the punishment of whipping and to have thirty stripes, and to be burnt in the cheek with the letter R and to work with a shakle on his legg for one whole year...and after his full time of service is Expired with his said master to serve the colony for seven whole years, and the said Peter Wilcocke to receive thirty stripes and to be Burnt in the cheek with the letter R...and the said Andrew Noxe to receive thirty stripes...and Emanuel the Negro to receive thirty stripes and to be burnt in the cheek with the letter R and to work in shakle one year or more as his master shall see cause..." 22nd July, 1640

Two cases before the courts in the same month involving English and African runaway servants. The case of July 22nd does show the court's impartiality in meting out the sentences, although severe. Four of the men – Christopher, Peter, Andrew, and Emanuel – all received thirty lashes, and Emanuel wasn't the only person receiving a branding of the letter "R" (Runaway) to his cheek – Christopher and Peter did as well. That was a horrible form of punishment. But the earlier case of July 9th revealed the beginning of something very sinister. All three men also received whippings for their crime. But for Victor the Dutchman, and James Gregory the Scotchman, their added punishment for running away was to merely serve one whole year apiece after the time of their current service expired. However, for the "Negro named John Punch" his additional sentence was:

"...serve his said master and his assigns **for the time of his natural Life here or elsewhere**"

John Punch (sometimes spelled Bunch) was sentenced to servitude for the rest of his life, and wherever he went. The ruling did not use the word "slave", but there was no question the Virginia Assembly had begun to legally define one. Another ruling was issued in 1642, aimed at the African community in the colony:

> "Be it also enacted and confirmed That there be tenn pounds of tob'o. per poll & a bushell of corne per poll paid to the ministers within the severall parishes of the collony for all tithable persons, that is to say, as well for all youths of sixteen years of age as upwards, as also for all negro women at the age of sixteen years"

Now the females of African descent sixteen years and up, would be taxed.

Here now comes the strange court case of the African, Anthony Johnson and his servant John Casor, as related in *The Journal of Negro History*, Volume I, June 1916, pages 233-237. Anthony Johnson was one of the Angolans who came in 1619. He later gained his freedom and married an African woman named Mary, who had been brought to Virginia sometime before 1623. They later moved to Northampton County, Virginia where Anthony had acquired 250 acres of land by 1651. Anthony had become so prosperous, he was able to import five indentured servants of his own. Because of this, he was granted the headrights to an additional 250 acres. A headright was a legal grant of land that the Virginia Company gave to any settler willing to pay the transportation costs for another person to be brought to Virginia. In turn, that person would become an Indentured servant in order to repay the landowner for the transportation costs. Landowners would receive 50 acres for each person brought over to expand the colony and the economy. Thus, many landowners and families grew in power by receiving large grants when they imported many servants and slaves. This also created an abuse of power, as the elite could be issued headrights of large tracts of land for fictitious people and falsifying the records. The number of headrights issued was four times more than the increase in population. The headrights system also kept many poor settlers from acquiring their own land, resulting in a sharecropper's arrangement, and strife between the rich and poor.

One of Anthony Johnson's servants was John Casor, also a person of African descent as Johnson, who said he had been imported for a seven or eight year term, and after serving that amount, claimed that Johnson would not allow his freedom. Johnson claimed that Casor did not have such a contract, but that he had Casor "for his life." Johnson let Casor go, upon the urgings of his family, and Casor went to work for another landowner named Robert Parker. Later, Johnson accused Parker of taking his worker and filed a lawsuit, *Johnson vs. Parker.* The Court made its ruling on March 8, 1654:

> "Whereas complaint was this daye made to ye court by ye humble peticion of Anth. Johnson Negro ag[ains]t Mr. Robert Parker that hee detayneth one John Casor a Negro the plaintiffs Serv[an]t under pretense yt the sd Jno. Casor is a freeman the court seriously considering & maturely weighing ye premises doe fynd that ye sd Mr. Robert Parker most unrightly keepeth ye sd Negro John Casor from his r[igh]t mayster Anth. Johnson as it appeareth by ye Deposition of Capt. Samll Gold smith & many probable circumstances. be it therefore ye Judgement of ye court & ordered that ye sd Jno. Casor negro, shall forthwith bee turned into ye service of his sd master Anthony Johnson and that the sd Mr. Robert Parker make payment of all charges in the suite and execution"

The Court did not grant Casor his freedom, but ruled that he be returned to the service of his master Anthony Johnson. The court, in effect, agreed with Johnson that Casor was his servant "for his life." Of course, Johnson could at any time release Casor from servitude and grant him freedom. But the point was, the court had given judicial sanction to the right of a "Negro" to own slaves of his own race for life. Thus, the courts were still perfecting and creating a legal basis and precedent for a lifetime servant or slave.

Then, in 1662, the word "slave" was used for the first time in Virginia law pertaining to persons of African descent in the colony:

> "WHEREAS some doubts have arrisen whether children got by any Englishman upon a negro woman should be **slave** or ffree, Be it therefore enacted and declared by this present grand assembly, that all children borne in this country shall be held bond or free only according to the condition of the mother, And that if any christian shall committ ffornication with a negro man or woman, hee or shee soe offending shall pay double the ffines imposed by the former act."

This statute also began to legally define and slowly create a new status in Virginian life, the slave. Any children born in the colony moving forward, would be either free or held bond, meaning slave, according to the condition of the mother. So if the mother was defined a slave, so would the child. This was totally contrary to English law. The Virginia colony followed English primogeniture law, generally defined as birth lineage by paternal acknowledgement, the father. But this statute circumvented that, transferring any entitlement to the legal status of the mother. Only if the mother was free, could the child be.

Interestingly, England had recently entered the Atlantic Slave Trade by about the 1640's with its keen interest in Barbados and the sugar production in the Caribbean. Even London opened a slave port in 1660. Also in the same year, the Virginia Assembly passed a statute in the colony entitled *"An Act for the Dutch and all other Strangers for Tradeing to this Place."* The Royal Crown, aiming to strengthen England's international commerce, prohibited Dutch ships from trading to the colony. However, this Virginia statute allowed Virginia planters to trade tobacco to the Dutch in exchange for "negro slaves."

Virginia had clearly shifted in its attitude and viewpoint towards the Free Africans and Indentured servants of color within the colony. Other statutes were passed to further cripple and define them. In 1667 was passed *"An act declaring that baptism of slaves doth not exempt them from bondage*:

> "WHEREAS some doubts have risen whether children that are slaves by birth, and by the charity and piety of their owners made pertakers of the blessed sacrament of baptisme, should by vertue of their baptisme be made free; It is enacted and declared by this grand assembly, and the authority thereof, that the conferring of baptisme doth not alter the condition of the person as to his bondage or ffreedome; that diverse masters, ffreed from this doubt, may more carefully endeavour the propagation of christianity by permitting children, though slaves, or those of greater growth if capable to be admitted to that sacrament"

The House of Burgesses decided that slaves born in Virginia would not become free even if they were baptized, as had been the custom before. In 1670 another statute passed, called *"Noe Negroes nor Indians to buy christian servants"* Act:

> "WHEREAS it hath beene questioned whither Indians or negroes manumited, or otherwise free, could be capable

of purchasing christian servants, It is enacted that noe negroe or Indian though baptised and enjoyned their owne
freedome shall be capable of any such purchase of christians,
but yet not debarred from buying any of their owne nation"

The wording of this statute implied that prior to its issuance,
"Negroes" and "Indians" *could* purchase persons of *any nationality*
within the colony for service. Otherwise, there would have been
no point in passing the ruling. The statute also made it clear that
"Christian servants" in the colony no longer included "Negroes" or
"Indians", even if they were baptized. The final four rulings between
1670 – 1705 would put the final nail in the coffin, and produce the
desired result for chattel slavery. In 1672 came the *Act for the apprehension and suppression of runaways, negroes, and slaves*:

"FORASMUCH as it hath beene manifested to this grand
assembly that many negroes have lately beene, and now are
out in rebellion in sundry parts of this country, and that
noe meanes have yet beene found for the apprehension and
suppression of them from whome many mischeifes of very
dangerous consequence may arise to the country if either
other negroes, Indians or servants should happen to fly
forth and joyne with them; for the prevention of which, be
it enacted by the governour, councell and burgesses of this
grand assembly, and by the authority thereof, that if any negroe, molatto, Indian slave, or **servant for life**, runaway and
shalbe persued by the warrant or hue and crye, it shall and
may be lawfull for any person who shall endeavour to take
them, upon the resistance of such negroe, molatto, Indian
slave, or servant for life, to kill or wound him or them soe
resisting; Provided alwayes, and it is the true intent and

meaning hereof, that such negroe, molatto, Indian slave, or servant for life, be named and described in the hue and crye which is alsoe to be signed by the master or owner of the said runaway. And if it happen that such negroe, molatto, Indian slave, or servant for life doe dye of any wound in such their resistance received the master or owner of such shall receive satisfaction from the publique for his negroe, molatto, Indian slave, or servant for life, soe killed or dyeing of such wounds; and the person who shall kill or wound by virtue of any such hugh and crye any such soe resisting in manner as aforesaid shall not be questioned for the same, he forthwith giveing notice thereof and returning the hue and crye or warrant to the master or owner of him or them soe killed or wounded or to the next justice of peace. And it is further enacted by the authority aforesaid that all such negroes and slaves shalbe valued at ffowre thousand five hundred pounds of tobacco and caske a peece, and Indians at three thousand pounds of tobacco and caske a peice, And further if it shall happen that any negroe, molatto, Indians slave or servant for life, in such their resistance to receive any wound whereof they may not happen to dye, but shall lye any considerable tyme sick and disabled, then alsoe the master or owner of the same soe sick or disabled shall receive from the publique a reasonable satisfaction for such damages as they shall make appeare they have susteyned thereby at the county court, who shall thereupon grant the master or owner a certificate to the next assembly of what damages they shall make appeare; And it is further enacted that the neighbouring Indians doe and hereby are required and enjoyned to seize and apprehend all runawayes whatsoever that

shall happen to come amongst them, and to bring them before some justice of the peace whoe upon the receipt of such
servants, slave, or slaves, from the Indians, shall pay unto
the said Indians for a recompence twenty armes length of
Roanoake or the value thereof in goods as the Indians shall
like of, for which the said justice of peace shall receive from
the publique two hundred and fifty pounds of tobacco, and
the said justice to proceed in conveying the runaway to his
master according to the law in such cases already provided;
This act to continue in force till the next assembly and noe
longer unlesse it be thought fitt to continue"

This statue defined four types of legal status for persons of
color: Negro and mulatto persons, which meant those who were free;
Indian slave, and *servant for life*. This ruling also made it legal to
wound or kill a person of color who resisted arrest, and for the owner
of any slave to be financially compensated. Next, the statute of 1680
restricted and policed the movements of slaves to meet at gatherings,
including funerals. It also became illegal to physically defend oneself
against unjust seizure. Next, the statute of 1691 was the first miscegenation law against interracial marriage. Other English colonies were
passing similar measures and statutes. The miscegenation law also
closed the loophole that the 1662 ruling did not close, that a child of
color would become a slave if the mother was a slave, but the child
would be free if the mother was English. Now, even if the mother was
a free English woman to a child of color, her child would be bound
out for thirty years.

Finally, in 1705 came several devastating enactments, including being denied the right to testify as witnesses in court, and declar-

ing "**the Negro, Mulatto, and Indian slaves within this dominion, to be real estate**."

Not to say that the lives of Indentured Servants had it any better before slavery was finally put in place legally. There are several accounts of Indentured servants, in particular Irish servants, being killed, beaten, and tortured at the hands of their masters. As was shown in the previous statute rulings, indentured servants from England and Scotland were taken advantage of, and received whippings, brandings, and all types of punishments.

As England entered the Atlantic Slave Trade, the need for Indentured Servants dried out, and was replaced by enslaved Africans. Their Virginian-born offspring were also stripped of their rights, even though they were born in a colony under the Royal Crown. Codified Slavery was now the law of the land, and would continue until the end of the American Civil War and the passage of the Civil Rights Act of 1866.

But just as with the case regarding the passage of the ban on the Trans-Atlantic Slave Trade in 1808, when those determined to keep Slavery alive found other means to keep people in oppression, so too, with the passage of the Civil Rights Act of 1866, as violent groups such as the Ku Klux Klan, the Redshirts, and the White League paved the way for the Compromise of 1877 and the removal of the last federal soldiers from the South, killing Reconstruction and giving birth to Jim Crow segregation.

CHAPTER 10

1626

When we talk about Slavery in New York, most people think of the slave market that was established on Wall Street in 1711. But the system of Slavery was much deeper than that. New York was an integral part of the Trans-Atlantic Slave Trade.

Before we remind ourselves the history of New York's role in the slave trade, let us look at how slavery first came to New York.

In the year 1626, at an area called *Mahattoe* by the aboriginal Lenape along the east bank of the Hudson River, eleven Africans from Central Africa were unloaded onto the harbor of a Dutch colony called New Amsterdam (New York City). These Africans, all males, were Paulo Angola, Big Manuel, Little Manuel, Manuel de Gerrit de Reus, Simon Congo, Antony Portuguese, Gracia, Piter Santomee, Jan Francisco, Little Antony, and Jan Fort Orange.

The men had been originally captured by the Portuguese, held in bonds at their slave-trade port Luanda, and loaded onto a Spanish slave ship heading to the Caribbean. However, a military ship belonging to the Dutch West India Company intercepted the Spanish slaver and stole the eleven men from it, holding the men against their will yet again.

The Dutch West India Company founded their permanent colony in an area called by the Lenape *Paggank* (nut island) in 1624, which later became the area of Albany, New York The Dutch named their colony New Netherland, the colony encompassing present-day New York, New Jersey, Delaware, Connecticut, and parts of Pennsylvania and Rhode Island. Actually, in 1613, a free black trader working for a Dutch fur trading company as a translator came to Manhattan Island from the Dominican. His name was Juan Rodrigues, who stayed in Manhattan and traded with the local Lenape on the island.

The Netherlands, who broke for their independence from the Spanish branch of the House of Habsburg in 1581, established the Dutch West India Company in 1621, for the purpose of carrying on economic warfare against Spain and Portugal. The company's charter was aimed toward Dutch interests in the Atlantic Slave Trade, Brazil, the Caribbean, and North America. The Dutch West India Company was actually a continuation of the *Dutch East Indies Company*, a corporation the Netherlands founded in 1602 to champion the Dutch war of independence from Spain.

Sometime later in the year 1626, after the eleven men from the Congo region had been brought to *Mahattoe* by the Dutch – who planned to use them for slave labor in their town New Amsterdam – the Dutch West India Company purchased 22, 000 acres – Mahattoe Island – from the Lenape people. One member of the Dutch company sent a letter to inform his government, The Netherlands, of the purchase:

"High and Mighty Lords,

Yesterday the ship the Arms of Amsterdam arrived here. It sailed from New Netherland out of the River Mauritius on the 23d of September. They report that our people are in good spirit and live in peace. The women also have borne some children there. They have purchased the Island Manhattes from the Indians for the value of 60 guilders. It is 11,000 morgens in size. They had all their grain sowed by the middle of May, and reaped by the middle of August. They sent samples of these summer grains: wheat, rye, barley, oats, buckwheat, canary seed, beans and flax...

In Amsterdam, the 5th of November anno 1626
Your High and Mightiness's obedient, P. Schaghen"

The changing faces of the aggressors upon the real estate of the indigenous in the Caribbean, Brazil, Haiti, Mexico, and other aboriginal homelands had now spilled over into the virgin lands along the Atlantic East Coast. The molding of the future "United States of AMERICA" was now in play, as Spain controlled Florida, England held Virginia, and the Dutch Netherlands claimed New York. Eventually, Great Britain would take over New York. In time, the Thirteen Colonies of the American Revolution would take its turn to govern. Would it do any better – allow ALL people freedom? History would answer that question in due time.

The year 1626 was indeed a history timeline marker, as the enslaved from Kongo who were imported into Manhattan, as well as the indigenous already there for generations, began laying the foundations for New York from their slave labor. It was also the beginning foundation for a "free Black community" that came into existence, even before slavery had yet to be abolished there.   In time, other kidnapped persons would come directly from Africa, the Caribbean, Brazil, and Curacao. In 1627, three enslaved women of color were brought to Manhattan Island. The name of one of them was Dorothy Creole.

The eleven Africans were then put to work by the Dutch West India Company. In time, other kidnapped persons would come directly from Africa, the Caribbean, Brazil, and Curacao. Yes, the Dutch Netherlands had now succumbed to the thirsty grab for wealth, power, and profit from the invaluable resource of human trafficking, by competing rivalries with Spain and Portugal.

Today, descendants of the eleven men brought in 1626 – as well as other enslaved persons of African descent who were later brought into New York – tell the stories that were passed down to them from their ancestors. The conditions and circumstances which led to a free African community emerging in New York City during Dutch rule (and later British and American rule) are documented.

The documents reveal, oddly, that even though Africans were being held against their will in the Dutch colony of New York, the Dutch style-of-rule still allowed enslaved persons their legal rights, and access to their judicial system. One example being on December 9, 1638, when Anthony the Portuguese, one of the eleven men, sued a white merchant for injury his dog caused to Anthony's hog. Anthony, a slave, was awarded damages. Another case involved Manuel de Reus, also of the eleven, who in 1639 was granted a power of attorney to collect his back wages from his employer. The colony's laws allowed enslaved Africans to legally marry, and own property, including land. They also were not prohibited from inter-racial marriage. The Dutch also made the provision for manumission, but in two phases: *conditional freedom*, and full freedom.

After serving the colony in Manhattan for eighteen years, the eleven Africans petitioned the courts for their release, claiming the Company had promised them freedom. The petition also stated their desire for liberty in order to care for their families. On February 25, 1644, the Dutch West India Company granted the men conditional freedom:

"We, Willem Kieft, director general, and the council of New Netherland, having considered the petition of the Negroes named Paulo Angola, Big Manuel, Little Manuel, Manuel de Gerrit de Reus, Simon Congo, Antony Portuguese, Gracia, Piter Santomee, Jan Francisco, Little Antony and Jan Fort Orange, who have served the Company for 18 or 19 years, that they may be released from their servitude and be made free."

Manumission of Manuel de Gerrit et al, 25 February 1644

The Company only granted the men conditional freedom, as long as they would pay yearly dues of "30 skepels of maize, wheat, peas or beans, and one fat hog," and to assist the Company when needed, or else face being re-enslaved. The Dutch company also granted them land. Other Africans were given freedom and granted parcels of land. In 1659 and 1660, the Company Director, Stuyvesant, granted more land lots to African-descent families in Manhattan. In 1662, the Company granted conditional freedom to three women. One of the women, named Mayken, just a few months later petitioned for full freedom. Mayken was granted her full freedom, after thirty-four years of being enslaved. On September 4, 1664, a petition for full freedom was presented from eight African men and filed with the Council. On December 21, 1664, these eight men were granted full freedom: Ascento Angola, Christoffel Santome, Pieter Pietersz Criolie, Antony Antonysz Criolie, Salomon Pietersz Criolie, Jan Guinea, Lowies Guinea, and Bastiaen Pietersz.

The freed Africans and their family heirs of descent created the first free Black community in Manhattan. The records show they cared for one another, as they strived to carve out a life of existence in this new village they had to accept as their new home. Anna van Angola was granted six acres. She had been widowed twice. Sebastiaen de Britto married Isabel Kisana, who was from Angola. They received land. Anthony Fernando Portuguese found a wife in 1642. A widow named Catalina received land. She had a two-year old child. Bastiaen d' Angola was given freedom in 1654. No strings were attached to his manumission, except "to gain a livelihood for himself, as any other free person may do." Willem Antonys Portuguese received land from his deceased father, Anthony Portuguese. Domingo Angola married a woman named Maycke. She later received a land grant. Manuel Trompeter's land was confirmed to his children Bernard and Christina. In 1663, Domingo Angola petitioned the Council that Manuel Trompeter's orphaned daughter Christina be granted her freedom, which was so orderd. Big Manuel's land went to his widow Christina de Angola. Paolo D'Angola's land went to his widow Dorothy Creole, one of the three women who arrived in 1627. Pieter Santome's land went to his sons Lucas and Salomon. Lucas was an apprentice in the barber trade. Little Anthony married Lucie d'Angola on May 5, 1641. They had a son, Anthony, in July 1643. However, Lucie died about four weeks later. The child Anthony was adopted by his godmother Dorothy, the wife of Paolo d'Angola. Anthony's father Little Anthony later died in 1648, and Dorothy's husband Paolo also died. In 1661, Dorothy and her new husband, Emanuel Pieters, petitioned the Council that their foster son Anthony "be declared by your noble honors to be a free person" so that "he could inherit by last will and testament." Freedom was awarded Anthony. He later received the land patent of his late father.

These families lived on their land in the town of Manhattan for generations as free people, as shown by an entry notated in the journal of Jasper Danckaerts:

"We went from the city, following the Broadway, over the _valley_, or the fresh water. Upon both sides of this way were many habitations of negroes, mulattoes and whites. These negroes were formerly the proper slaves of the (West India) company, but, in consequence of the frequent changes and conquests of the country, **they have obtained their freedom** and settled themselves down where they have thought proper, and thus on this road, where they have ground enough to live on with their families. We left the village, called the Bowery, lying on the right hand, and went through the woods to New Harlem, a tolerably large village situated on the south side of the island..."

Journal of Jasper Danckaerts, 1679 – 1680

According to his description of the Manhattan, New York neighborhood, we can decipher the neighborhood is in present-day Greenwich Village.

The British would soon take over New York, a change of government in New Amsterdam, which would have reverberating effects on the people of color on Manhattan Island for several decades. On August 27, 1664, four military ships of war from England sailed into New Amsterdam's harbor and demanded the Dutch colony of New Netherlands to surrender. The articles of surrender were soon signed in September 1664. As the British and Dutch were preparing for official transfer of power, the Dutch Company Director, Stuyvesant, fearing that the people of color might never claim their freedom under the new British government, began freeing as many enslaved people of color as he could within days of the transfer. Land was also granted as previously discussed.

After the British took control of New York, slavery was legalized, and slave codes were put into effect. Another change was – unlike Dutch rule which allowed people of color access to the judicial system and allowed a measure of legal rights – no rights were allowed anyone who was labeled a "slave." The British did tolerate former manumissions under the Dutch, however. But any "slip of the law" for a free person of color could mean being sold back into slavery in New York.

In 1711, a slave market was formally opened at the end of Wall Street, where enslaved persons could be hired out. More on Wall Street later. The next year, 1712, a revolt against slavery broke out, killing 8 whites and 25 blacks.

Slavery in New York by 1730 had become so systematic and controlling that "An Act for the more effectual preventing and punishing the conspiracy and insurrection of Negro and other slaves and for better regulating them" was passed, prohibiting an assembly of three or more people of color:

> "Foresmuch as the number of slaves in the cities of New York and Albany, as also within the several couties, towns and manors within this colony doth daily increase, and that they have oftentime been guilty of confederating together in running away, and of other ill and dangerous practices, it is unlawful for above three slaves to meet together at any time, or at any other place than when it shall happen they meet in some servile employment for their masters' or mistresses' profit, and by their masters' or mistresses' consent, upon penalty of being whipt upon the naked back, at the discretion of any one justice of the piece [sic], not exceeding forty lashes"

Another ordinance was enacted in 1737, "A Law for Regulating Negro's & Slaves in the Night Time", which made it unlawful to:

"That no Negro, Mulatto or Indian Slave, shall appear in the Streets of this City, above an hour after Sun-set without a candle and Lanthorn, on penalty of being Whipt at the Publick Whipping Post."

In 1741, another revolt against slavery rose up, which lasted for six months.

Today, some say the only reminder of New York City's participation in the slave trade is a small plaque posted at the bottom of Wall Street and was dedicated in 2015. In 1711, a slave market was formally opened at the end of Wall Street. It started as a wooden fence that enslaved people were directed to build in 1653, then in 1685 it became a street barricade which crossed an indigenous trail path (the path later became Broadway Street). Wall Street served as a marketplace where enslaved persons would be hired out.

But people today may not realize how much of an integral role New York City played in slavery. On March 2, 1807, the House and Senate of the United States agreed on a bill called "*An Act to prohibit the importation of slaves into any port or place within the jurisdiction of the United States, from and after the first day of January, in the year of our Lord, One Thousand Eight Hundred and Eight.*" President Thomas Jefferson signed the bill into law. Many believed this would put an end to America's involvement in the international slave trade, and that slavery would dry up in the South.

But the Trans-Atlantic Slave Trade continued *illegally* in America after January 1808, and right up until the Civil War. Most of us have heard about the *Clotilda* slave ship that sailed illegally into Mobile, Alabama in 1860, with 110 kidnapped from Dahomey, West Africa, in the Bight of Benin. However, there were way more illegal slave ships that arrived besides *Clotilda*. After 1808, some 8,000 African captives were brought by slave traders into the American South, with New York City playing a key role.

A group of twelve investment slave traders known as the Portuguese Company set up an office in Manhattan in the early 1850's and began buying ships to send to Africa for slaves. Soon Baltimore, Boston, New Orleans, and other American ports became involved in the operation. When Cuba became a part of the United States, the Manhattan operations expanded and soon enslaved persons were being sent to Cuba. Britain was frustrated. Although British navy patrols were seizing slave ships from other countries in the Atlantic, they had no authority at that time to seize American ships.

Britain actually sent undercover spies to Manhattan, New York to gather intelligence on slave trading. British spy Emilio Sanchez reported that American clearance clerks with Customs were also involved, looking the other way, and being bought off to conceal when slavers were leaving port. Some of the associates of the Portuguese Company were reported carrying suitcases full of cash.

Two such slavers that left New York harbor were the brig *Julia Moulton* and the schooner *Wanderer*. In 1854, the *Julia Moulton* left New York to Africa and then was seized after landing in Cuba. The ship captain was merely fined, and was later pardoned by President Buchanan. The schooner *Wanderer* was originally built in New York in 1857 as a pleasure ship, but later bought by a Southern businessman and an investment group. The ship passed New York's harbor inspection, headed to the Congo in 1858 and upon arriving, shelves and pens were built and fitted into the hold. Then 487 slaves were loaded. *Wanderer* landed at Jekyll Island, Georgia on November 28, 1858 with 409 slaves who had survived the passage. The enslaved were then shipped to Savannah and Augusta, Georgia, South Carolina, Florida, and Mississippi.

Slavery in New York was said to have been abolished on July 4, 1827. While that may have been true inside New York itself, the aforementioned facts show that New York City was keeping Slavery alive and well in other places.

In 1780, during the American Revolutionary War, about 10,000 people of African descent lived in New York City. This was in part to the British announcing freedom to any enslaved persons who left their American masters and come to the British side. Thousands came. One of them was a sixteen-year-old girl named Deborah Squash, a runaway from George Washington's slaves. Another person who made their way to New York was Boston King, who had been enslaved in South Carolina before he ran away. The war ended in 1781, and negotiations began between the two governments in Paris, France, where a treaty was drafted on November 30, 1782 and signed on September 3, 1783. However, during April – September 1783, representatives of Great Britain and the United States met at a tavern in Manhattan to compile a roll of names to former enslaved persons who wished to evacuate with the British rather than remain in New York. Known as the *Book of Negroes*, the official title was also called "Inspection Roll of Negroes New York, New York City Book No. 1 April 23 – September 13, 1783." The tavern where the list was compiled – Queens Head Tavern – was owned by a free black named Samuel Fraunces. Today the tavern is located on Pearl Street in Manhattan. About 3,000 persons of British loyalists are named, of whom the United States argued for the return of their "property", but British commander Guy Carlton refused, saying it would be "A dishonorable violation of public faith" to not keep their promise to those who wished to leave New York with them. The evacuation took place on November 25, 1783. The three thousand loyalists of African descent ended up resettling in various places. Many went to Nova Scotia and the West Indies, others to London, and several to Sierra Leone, where they founded Freetown in 1792. Deborah Squash, and her husband Harvey, went to Nova Scotia. Boston King also went there, and then later he settled in Sierra Leone.

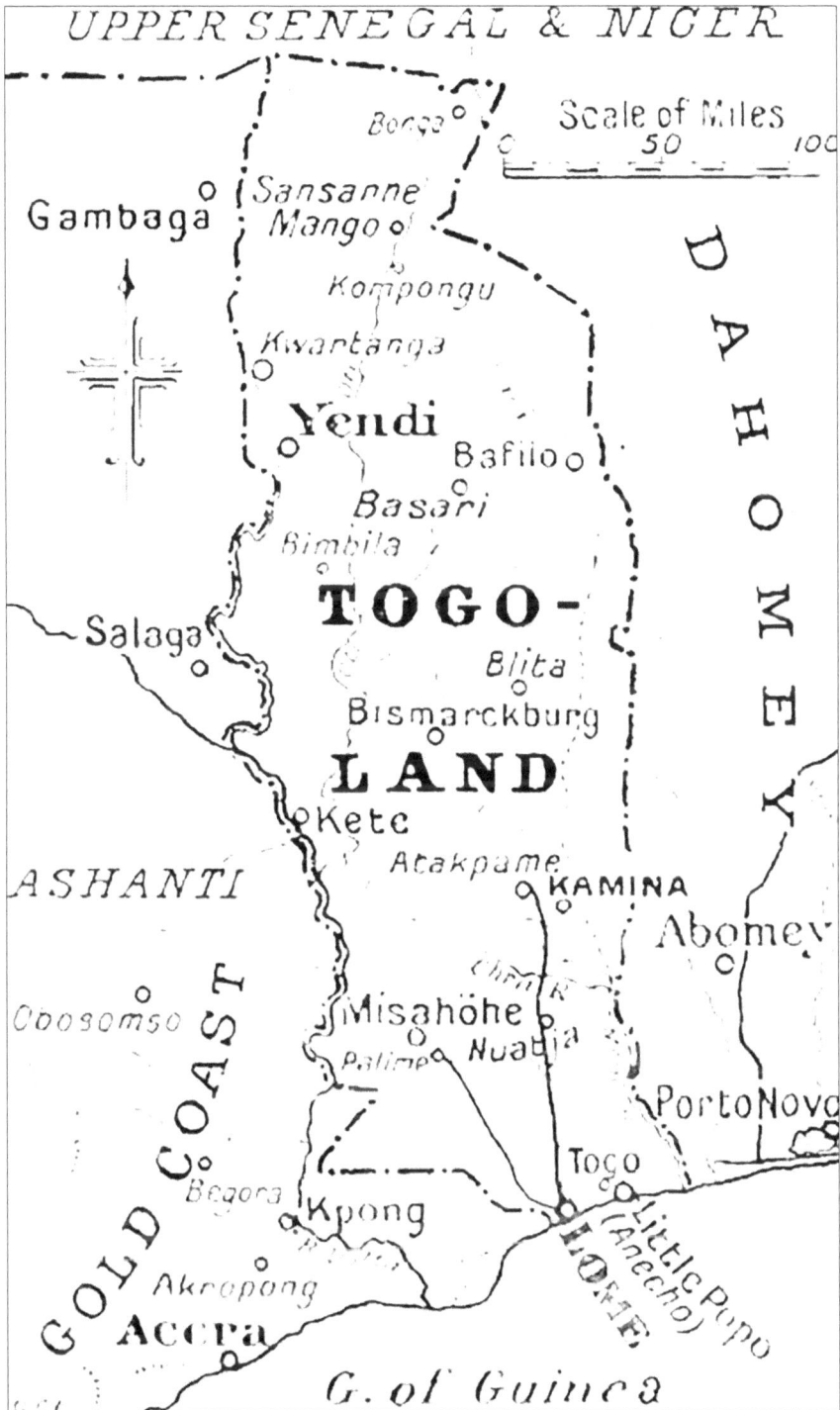

Map of Togoland, 1914, the Slave Coast

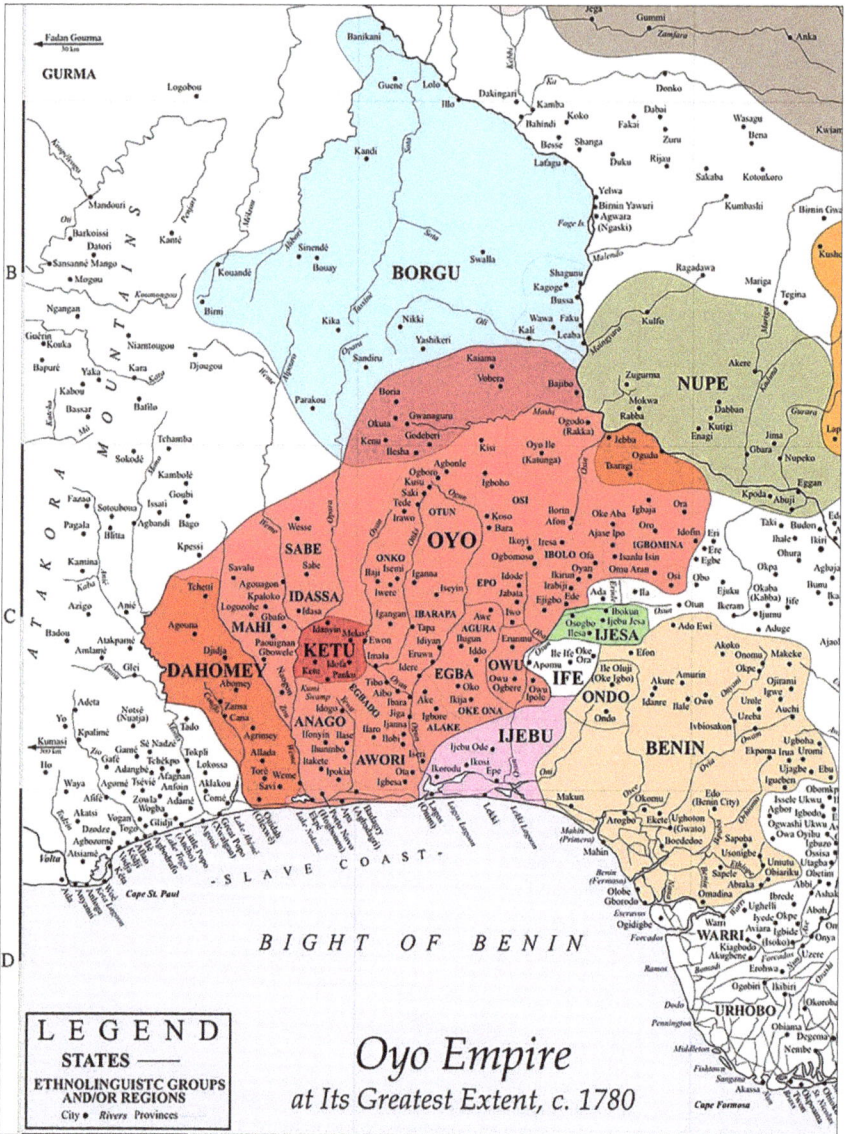

Map of the Oyo Empire, Bight of Benin

Pope Nicholas V, Bishop of Rome

Whore of Babylon, from Martin Luther's 1534 translation of the Bible

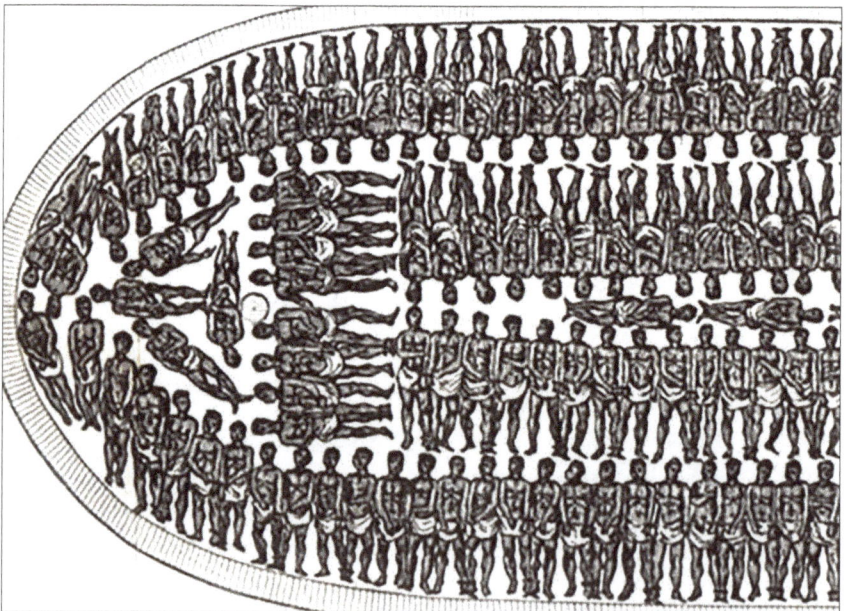

African Slave Ship Cargo. The Trans-Atlantic Slave Trade continued into America until the Civil War

First Slave Auction, 1655, New Amsterdam (New York)

Land of the Jews, 1588, by Livio Sanuto

Bambara Territory, West Africa, 1819, by Thomas Bowdich

JEWISH NEGROES.

The Rev. Dr. Phillip, missionary in the north of Africa, gives the following details concerning that country. A Russian Jew, resident at Meadah, gave him information concerning a great number of Israelites inhabiting the oases of Sahara, and dwelling also at Buthhor, Bis-Wrabi, Tauggurt, Bousra, Bein Uzab Loquas, etc. There are in each of these places even more. In one place he found six hundred fami-lies, with numerous synagogues, and about a ment, some of which were more ancient than __ __ __ and ever seen.

But this is not all; other curious details reached Dr. Phillip from another source. A Jew, who had accompanied a German traveller as far as Timbuctoo, found near the boundary of Bambara a large number of Jewish negroes. Nearly every family among them possesses the law of Moses, written upon parchment. Al-though they speak of the prophets, they have not their writings. Their prayers differ from those of other Jews, and are committed to little leaves of parchment, stitched together, and con-tain numerous passages derived from the Psalms.

These Jews have mingled some of the super-stitions of "oral Law" (which they have not committed to writing,) with those of their neigh-bors, the Mahomedans and the heathen. They enjoy equal liberty with the other subjects of the African chiefs, and have their synagogues and their rabbis. The explanation which they give of themselves, in connection with their black skin, is this—that after the destruction of Jerusalem, at the time of the captivity, some of their ancestors, having neither goods nor land, fled to the desert. The fatigue which they endured was so great, that nearly all the females died by the way. The children of Ham received them with kindness, and by inter-mar-riage with their daughters, who were black,

North Carolina Newspaper Article in 1853, Negro Jews

Wrabi, Tauggurt, Bousra, ~~Deni Colo Loquan,~~
etc. There are in each of these places even
more. In one place he found six hundred families, with numerous synagogues, and about a
ment, some of which were more ancient than
~~...had ever seen.~~

But this is not all; other curious details
reached Dr. Phillip from another source. A
Jew, who had accompanied a German traveller
as far as Timbuctoo, found near the boundary
of Bambara a large number of Jewish negroes.
Nearly every family among them possesses the
law of Moses, written upon parchment. Although they speak of the prophets, they have
not their writings. Their prayers differ from
those of other Jews, and are committed to little
leaves of parchment, stitched together, and con-
tain numerous passages derived from the
Psalms.

These Jews have mingled some of the super-
stitions of "oral Law" (which they have not
committed to writing,) with those of their neigh-
bors, the Mahomedans and the heathen. They
enjoy equal liberty with the other subjects of
the African chiefs, and have their synagogues
and their rabbis. The explanation which they
give of themselves, in connection with their
black skin, is this—that after the destruction
of Jerusalem, at the time of the captivity, some
of their ancestors, having neither goods nor
land, fled to the desert. The fatigue which
they endured was so great, that nearly all the
females died by the way. The children of Ha...

North Carolina Newspaper Article, the Bambara

CHAPTER 11

Free People of Color, Melungeons, Greeks, Hebrews

Who are the descendants of those who came in 1619? Who were the free generations of **the Free People Of Color** before 1705 (before Legal Slavery was then officially "Locked In," and became the law of the land in America)? **Where are the descendants of the enslaved Hebrews who came to America?**

As the slave laws in the Colony of Virginia continued to expand, it also continued to restrict the African community. Whereas before, the social rank in Colonial Virginian society was based on one's Class – Gentleman, Planter, Nobleman, Indentured Servant, and being "Christian" – it now began radically shifting to one's *Race*; And, this shift towards emphasizing *Race* would affect the ability to self-determine one's own legal and economic status. It would spell the difference between being free or being enslaved.

Many "Free Colored Negro" and "Free Mulatto" families began moving to other English colonies and newer places to acquire land, property, and better opportunities. Some moved to Maryland. Others went to the colonies of North and South Carolina. Yet others made their way to the Territory of Tennessee. For example, "Free Negro" John Johnson Jr., the grandson of the Anthony *Johnson vs. Parker* court case (see Chapter 9), moved to Maryland and bought about 50 acres of land in 1675. Johnson called his farm "Angola." Another example showing the migration of Free families were the family names Collins, Bunch, and Gibson from Louisa County, Virginia who show up together in various counties of North Carolina (See Chapter 6). Still others moved to French/Spanish Louisiana and remained there even after the United States purchased Louisiana.

In July 2005, a study called the Melungeon DNA Project was launched, with the purpose of studying and identifying the ancestry of a group of families with noted dark countenance who had migrated from Virginia to the eastern portions of Tennessee, namely the Hancock and Hawkins County areas. These groups of families were known as "Melungeon" by the local community. According to their published paper in 2012 "*Melungeons, A Multi-Ethnic Population,* the historical notes made by a local attorney in Hancock County named Lewis Jarvis about the Melungeon families were studied from an article he had written in 1903. Here is a portion of what Jarvis wrote:

> "They settled here in 1804, possibly about the year 1795... friendly Indians who came with the whites as they moved west. They came from Cumberland County and New River, Va., stopping at various points west of the Blue Ridge. Some of them stopped on Stony Creek, Scott County, Virginia where Stony Creek runs into Clinch River...many of these friendly Indians live in the mountains of Stony Creek, but they have married among the whites until the race has almost become extinct..."

The Melungeon DNA Project's report makes mention of Jarvis again in a letter he wrote in 1914 to the wife of John Trotwood Moore, the Tennessee State Librarian and Archivist, about these families of color at Stoney Creek, Virginia. Jarvis says:

"The name Melungeon was given them" because of "their color."

The surnames "Goins, Sweat, Bunch, Collins, Gibson, Chavis, Keys, Kersey, and many more, were family names that early African and Mulatto families had adopted, going back to the history of Colonial America. Of course, these particular names were also held by English colonists too. Those names originated from England and other European locations. But at the same time, *these surnames also became like a branding signature to families of African descent in early America.* A sampling of some noted family names comprising mixed African, Indian, & European Blood descent in early colonial America were: Adkins, Ailstock, Banks, Bass, Bunch, Cannady, Chavis, Collins, Cornish, Driggers, Evans, Gibson, Goins/Goings, Gowen, Grantham, Herring, Ivey/Ivie/Ivy, James, Johnson, Kersey, Moore, Mullins, Perkins, Robertson, Robinson, Sweat, Tann, Tate, Turner, Williams (Sources, Chapter 11).

What is also interesting about Lewis Jarvis' notes is what he said *why* the name "Melungeon" was used on the families who had settled in his Tennessee county from Virginia. He said the name Melungeon was given them *"on account of their color."* Where did the name Melungeon come from, and what was the meaning of the name? We shall discuss that shortly.

While several descendants of the 1619 Africans migrated north, south, and west, **others stayed in Virginia.** One such family were the Going/Goin descendants of ancestor Christopher Gowen, born around 1658. **Some researchers say that Christopher Gowen was another son of Mihil (or Michael) Gowen, one of the first generation Africans in Virginia.** In 1679, Christopher's wife Anne Gowen gave birth to a son in Gloucester County, and was *named Michael.*

By 1702, the family was now living in New Kent County, along with *another young male named Philip*, born around 1685. It is very possible that the two boys Michael and Philip were named after Mihil (Michael) Gowen and Philip Gowen, who we recall had both been bound as "Negro" servants for Amy Barnhouse's family.

Christopher and Anne's son Philip Gowen of New Kent County probably was the father of George Gowen, born about 1715, when Philip Gowen was about twenty-five years of age. George Gowen may have been a brother, or closely related, to Agnes Gowen, a Free woman of Color born around 1725, as we shall see. George Gowen later married, and his wife Sarah gave birth to Aaron Gowen on the 9th of June 1737 in New Kent County. As for Agnes Gowen, she later moved to Louisa County. On the 9th of January 1743, Agnes "Going" was charged by the court for having an illegitimate child. She had given birth to a boy, Moses, in 1742. *Agnes was sentenced to receive twenty-five lashes on her back.*

Agnes went on to have nine other children. Besides Moses, were: Joseph, David, Sarah, Benjamin, Joshua, Elizabeth, Sherrod (Sherwood), Milly, and Usly. In November 1759, Agnes bound out her son Joseph and eight-year old daughter Sarah to James Bunch of Fredericksville Parish, Albemarle County. On May 14, 1770, the court ordered the churchwardens of Trinity Parish to indenture all of Agnes' children under twenty-one years except the youngest. Earlier, Agnes' son Moses and George Gowen's son Aaron were both named in court proceedings in Goochland County involving Thomas Underwood in September 1764. Moses acknowledged a debt of 15 pounds & 12 shillings to Underwood, and Aaron, when he was living in Louisa County, had mortgaged his household goods to Underwood for 36 pounds. **This fact establishes that the two young men, Moses Gowen and Aaron Gowen, knew each other. Both had the same** last name, which also indicated they were more than likely related. This, in turn, meant that their respective parents, George Gowen and Agnes Gowen, were also related as well.

In February 1765, George Gowen and his wife Sarah sued a Thomas Whitlock for trespass, assault, and battery. Whitlock, in turn, sued Sarah Gowen for a debt owed him. The court then ordered the sheriff to seize nine pigs belonging to Sarah and sell them to satisfy the debt. On July 14, 1777, Moses Gowen, along with two others, was charged by the Louisa County Court for hog stealing. The sheriff went out to arrest Moses and the two others, but was unable because they were in hiding.

By 1810, most of Agnes "Goings" adult children and grandchildren were now living in Albemarle County, except for her son Moses and her daughter Sarah. Moses and Aaron Gowen had gone to live in Powhatan County. Sarah Gowen had moved to Campbell County, where on May 12, 1802, she registered as a "Free Negro…5 feet 8 inches, 45 years old, Malattoe, born free in Louisa County." Agnes' son Benjamin Goings later died in 1822, and his Last Will and Testament named his wife Betty, his sons Daniel, James, & Jesse, and his daughters Mary Brock, Susan, Nelly, & Nancy. Agnes' son Sherrod Goings died in 1837, leaving his adult children and wife Susan. Some from this branch of the Goings/Goins later moved to Ohio. Sherrod and Susan Goings' daughter Ann, her husband John (or Jonathan) Goings, and their daughter Eliza Jane with her husband Joshua Goings **moved to Athens County, Ohio by 1857.**

Another related family, Walker and Mary Jane Goins, along with Mary's parents, Wilson Middlebrook and Nancy Goings, also left Virginia and headed to Athens County, Ohio by 1856. Some have wondered who were the parents of Walker Goins, who married Mary Jane Goings on the 23rd of August, 1848 in Albemarle

County, since no record has thus far turned up to reveal the answer. Based on my research, I have strong reason to believe Walker's father was a Benjamin Goins, born about 1801, who worked as a cooper in Albemarle and Augusta Counties. One reason being the marriage record book, citing Walker and Mary Jane's marriage, recorded three other names – Mary's father Wilson Goings who gave consent, Wilson's brother Joshua Goings who posted bond (Wilson also had a son named Joshua), and a Benjamin Goins as a witness. Benjamin Goins and his sister Anaca "Goings" were listed on the 1850 Federal Census, living right next to five other Goings families, including Shrerod Goings' daughter Agnes Goings, born about 1815. But, Walker and Mary Jane Goins are not listed in Benjamin Goins' household. In fact, Walker Goins, born about 1820, appears nowhere on either the 1840 or 1850 Virginia census, and doesn't show up as a head of household until the 1860 Ohio census. Furthermore, Benjamin Goins does not appear as a head of household on the 1840 Virginia census.

So who was the Benjamin Goins who appeared as a witness for Walker Goins' marriage in 1848? Was he a son to one of Agnes Goings' ten children? Her son Sherrod Goings died in 1837. His widow Susan Goings is listed as a head of household in 1840 in Fredericksville, Albemarle County, with eight other persons living with her. When comparing all the Goings listed on the 1840 census in Albemarle County, Susan Goings' household is the only one that matches the age range for Benjamin and Walker Goins. (It seems to me that Walker Goins, and very likely his father Benjamin Goins, came from the same family as Agnes Goings and her ten children, and hence, from the same Angolan ancestors. As a final side note, Sherrod and Susan Goings' daughter Agnes had a minor son and daughter named Silas and Harriet on the 1850 Albemarle County census. Walker and Mary Goins had two minor children with the same names on the 1860 Ohio census).

The question that still needs to be answered is, **why were several families who were of dark complexion claiming "Portuguese ancestry" when the courts became suspicious about their race?** A few examples of such cases have been provided in this book. But there are several more such cases of persons who declared Portuguese ancestry to legal U.S. courts and official census enumerators during the time of slavery and the Indian genocide. What is fascinating too, is that the majority of such declarations during that time period were from persons or families whose roots pointed back to early colonial Virginia. *Dna test results taken by their descendants today point to haplogroups of sub-Saharan African origin.*

This is not to say that every person or family who gave testimony of Portuguese lineage was incorrect. Some very well in fact might have been. But the main point of this discussion is to state that many who were of dark complexion and claimed Portuguese descent were of Sub-Sahara African origin, as DNA testing is now revealing. There is testimony about one person who claimed Portuguese descent and yet his claim was denied. This was during the 1874 Chattanooga, Tennessee court trial involving Martha Bolton, and whether she should be barred from inheriting her father's estate because her mother had been a woman of color. Testimony was given by Drury Dobbins Scruggs about Martha's grandfather Spencer Bolton, who claimed his lineage was Portuguese. But the part of Scruggs' testimony that is revealing is the words he said at the end:

"…at the same time my attention was also called in an official capacity to a Mr. Dempsey who claimed to be a Portuguese, and the decision in his case was that he was of mixed blood, but I gave him the right of appeal but he left the country."

Mr. Dempsey's claim of being Portuguese was denied because it was determined he had *mixed blood*, meaning "Negro." Mr. Dempsey may have been "Balum Dempsey," a mulatto shoemaker listed on the 1850 Spartanburg County, South Carolina census. Nonetheless, this example in 1874 shows that a person of color claimed a Portuguese lineage, and was aware of the benefits if successful in doing so, that it would immediately change his legal and free status in the Jim Crow south after Reconstruction. This also inferred that other People of Color were probably attempting the same. It is ironic that today's DNA testing is revealing the descendants of those early Kongo and Mbundu people who were brought to Colonial Virginia, many who actually were exposed to the Portuguese culture back home in Kongo, before the Portuguese wars captured them to be sold into slavery.

As those Congolese and their children and grandchildren began to painfully experience how the new Virginia slave laws were shackling and restricting their freedoms and movement, they were forced to come up with new strategies for them and their families to survive. For some, it meant moving to free States. For others, it meant holding on to one's "Free Negro" registration papers and forever remain in the community they were known in. For still others, it meant migrating to a remote area and learn to "Pass," either as "White" or as "Portuguese." Yet for many others, it meant not being able to escape the ultimate fate – being captured. No doubt, Kongo and Mbundu families in Virginia passed down to their children the history of their people, and how the Portuguese brought religion first; then trade, commerce, and culture came next; followed by the soldiers who came last. Perhaps that oral story was told over and over so often that in time, later children may have grew up believing that they actually were of Portuguese ancestry.

Where did the word "Melungeon" originally come? Before slavery began in the American colonies, enslaved Africans were being sent to the Caribbean and "New Spain" Mexico. Africans from Angola being sent to Brazil used a word in the Kimbundu and Kikongo languages to describe themselves – malungu, or malungo – which literally means "Great Canoe" or "companion in misfortune", but in Brazil the word was expanded to mean "shipmates." A British planter in Brazil during the 1800's named Henry Koster noted that Africans who were on the same slave ships together called each other *malungos*, and the bond formed between each other was considered just as important as the bond with their wives and children. Researcher and writer Tim Hashaw mentions the word "malungo" appears in a Portuguese Dictionary dating to 1779, with the example cited in the dictionary as: "malungo – the black calls another captive who came with him on the same ship." When the Africans from Angola began coming to Virginia, they also began using the word malungo (or melungo, as the Portuguese spelled the word). Over time, the word was corrupted into *melungeon*. Some say the family name Goins/Goings/Geons came from the last four letters of the word, and was originally used as the family name so they would always be reminded of where their roots came from. (Other researchers have totally different theories on the word melungeon). According to *The SAGE Encyclopedia of African Cultural Heritage in North America,* by Mwalimu J. Shujaa and Kenya J. Shujaa, it states the word "Malungu" came to be used as a self ascribed ethnic term identifying Bantu-speaking captives, and expanded to mean "shipmates."

What can we take away from this discussion about the first-generation Africans – the Congolese – who came to America in 1619 and for several decades thereafter? Several things. First, in the early history of this country, legalized slavery did not exist. Second, as time went on, laws were passed to create codified slavery, which also included the Native Indigenous, as their lands were illegally occupied, soon reduced to Reservations, and thousands forced to Oklahoma. The rights of all females and Indentured servants fared no better. But soon a distinction was made between black male and female servants and whites.

And third, we also saw the origins of the Free people of Color – Free Blacks and Mulattos of African and mixed descent and their descendants – who migrated all across America, **and who had already intermarried into many family names today whose roots go back to the American Revolution and even beyond to colonial times.**

So as we have seen, the Melungeons' roots go back to the first Africans of Virginia. As cited in his book's introduction, renowned genealogist Paul Heinegg in his book *Free African Americans of North Carolina and Virginia* stated that historians overlooked the colonial history of the FPOC American families, at the time his book was published in 1997. Heinegg makes a point in his book that may help us understand the impact of the Free People of Color in the context of the Melungeons. He stated that the light-skinned descendants of these families formed "tri-racial" communities stretching across the South. Therefore, the migrations of these tri-racial communities were not confined to just Virginia and Tennessee.

The first enslaved Africans arriving at Florida was in late 1526 (when Florida was under Spain), as a significant part of the expedition of Lucas Vazquez de Ayllon, who brought as many as 100 enslaved. (Earlier in 1521, Vazquez de Ayllon made landfall at Winyah Bay, South Carolina and seized seventy indigenous persons to be taken to Haiti as slave labor). But in less than two months from first arriving in 1526, his settlement in *La Florida* was abandoned due to disease, mutiny, and a slave rebellion, which burned down the house to one of the leaders. Legend claims the Africans who escaped, later joined with the local aboriginal Guale tribe.

The Melungeons: Congolese, Angolan, Portuguese, Indigenous North American, Spanish, British. What about Greeks? Consider the island of Crete.

Crete, the largest and most populous of the Greek islands in the Mediterranean Sea. It was the center of Europe's first advanced civilization, the Minoans. But who were the early Neolithic influences on the Minoans? One of them was Egypt. Minoan craftsmen were employed by Egypt to paint frescoes at Avaris, Egypt, discovered in the palace district at Tell el-Dab'a, and dating back to at least the 18th Dynasty of Egypt (1550 - 1292 BCE) or earlier. These wall paintings indicate international relations and cultural exchanges between early Crete and Egypt. Other researchers point to even earlier trade relations with Egypt (around 2300 BCE) with the invention of masted ships. Does the Bible shed light on the connection between the Greek island of Crete and Africa? Absolutely it does, in the following biblical texts.

First, in listing the Genealogy of Noah's son Ham, the Hebrew Bible says "And the sons of Ham were Cush and **Mizriam** and Put and Canaan" (Genesis 10:6). Now notice what the Bible says about the sons of Mizriam:

> "And Mizriam became father to Ludim and Anamim and Lehahim and Naphtuhim and Pathrusim and **Casluhim (from among whom the Philistines went forth)** and Caphtorim." (Genesis 10:13, 14)

So Mizriam (whose name means "Egypt" in Hebrew) had a son named **Casluhim, who was the forefather of the "Philistines,"** a people in biblical times who inhabited the ancient land of Canaan, on the coast of the Mediterranean between Joppa and Gaza. But where did the Philistines live before they lived in the land of Canaan? Notice what the Jewish prophet Yeremiah once said about the Philistines in a warning: "For Yahuah is despoiling the Philistines, who are <u>the remaining ones from the island of Caphtor</u>." (Jeremiah 47:4)

The identification of the "island of Caphtor" has been in debate. However, most scholars today are in general agreement that this text is referring to the island of Crete, off the coast of Greece, and of its neighboring islands and coastlands. Hence, the Philistines – descendants of Mizraim (Egypt) – apparently settled in the Greek island of Crete, prior to their later migration to Canaan by the time Abraham was reported to have run into them in the 20th Century BCE when he crossed the Euphrates.

So yes, Grecian and Mizraim DNA are entwined, going back much further than the Ptolemy period in Egypt, and could be considered another aspect of the Melungeon – Slave trade discussion.

Today, many White Americans who claim Melungeon ancestry are surprised in discovering African roots in their DNA testing. The result: many are learning the history of early America.

Even prominent names are showing DNA connections to the Free Africans of Virginia and their descendants. For example, a news release in 2012 from a popular DNA testing company announced that President Barack Obama is related to one of the first African families of Virginia, not through his Kenyan father, **but through his white mother.** Obama's mother descends from the African John Punch, the indentured servant in 1640 who was caught as a runaway and punished to serve his master "for his natural life" (See Chapter 9).

The servant Punch was still allowed to marry and have children. One of his children changed the last name to "Bunch," and that branch of the family migrated to Tennessee, where a daughter named Anna was born. This person had a daughter named Frances Allred in 1834, who later moved to Kansas. Four generations later, Obama's mother was born. Another celebrity's DNA result was publicized, this time on a popular genealogy TV broadcast, showing his connection to the early Africans in America, comedian and actor Chris Tucker, whose DNA test scored a high percentage rate of ancestry from the Mbundu people in Angola. And still yet, a news article quoted actor Johnny Depp as saying his ancestor of African descent was Elizabeth Key, the first documented female servant to sue for her freedom in Virginia and win, in 1660.

Enslaved people who won court victories during the time of Slavery were rare. Even the several struggles for freedom, which American historians label as "Insurrections" or "Rebellions," rarely ended in victorious liberty for the enslaved. The Stono "Rebellion" that took place in the colony of South Carolina in 1739 near the Stono River is one such example. The colony had been importing hundreds of enslaved Africans from the Kongo kingdom region of Central Africa. One of them was a man named Jemmy (history also names him 'Cato"). Being that there was no law at the time outlawing slaves from reading and writing, Jemmy was able to become literate in the use of English while a slave. Reports had been heard from the surrounding area that Spanish Florida offered freedom to any slave escaping British colonies and came to their borders. Spain allowed this as an attempt to destabilize British rule. Soon, Jemmy had recruited about twenty others of his Kongolese countrymen, and on September 9, 1739, they escaped and set out on a road toward Spanish Florida, recruiting more slaves until their number swelled to about 81. They burned down six plantations, and carried a banner that read "Liberty", at the same time shouting the word in unison. However, Jemmy's army didn't make it to Florida. The Lieutenant Governor's militia caught up with them the next day and ended that struggle for freedom. There were deaths on both sides. **After that struggle, South Carolina passed the Act of 1740, outlawing enslaved persons to learn** *to write.* The Act was later amended to also outlaw reading. Other colonies had similar laws. By 1834, there were anti-literacy laws throughout the Southern States.

Other court cases stand out that illustrate the rarity of court victories for FPOC. Take for example, the Gibson family. Some descend from Elizabeth Chavis, who had a child named Gibson in the 1600's in Virginia.

But the branch of the family who descended from ancestor Jane Gibson, sadly illustrate the thin line existing between freedom and slavery. Jane Gibson was born about 1640, lived in Charles City County, Virginia, and passed away around 1723. Jane Gibson had a free son George and free daughter Jane (born say 1662), who married free black Morris Evans. Jane and Morris Evans had a free daughter Frances Evans (born say 1685). Frances Evans had a daughter also named Frances, who was bound out by her mother to a Mr. Lightfoot in New Kent County. However, Mr. Lightfoot sold the daughter Frances into slavery. Frances later had a daughter named Sarah Colley and two granddaughters Hannah Evans (born say 1740) and Amey Evans (born say 1745). But if matters couldn't get any worse, Frances' master sold her daughter Sarah to one slave holder, sold her granddaughter Hannah to another man and sold her granddaughter Amey to yet another man, David Allen of Mecklenburg County, Virginia.

However, ancestor Jane Gibson's descendants put up a fight for their freedom. The children of Hannah Evans and Amey Evans turned to the legal courts to seek their release from slavery. Here is a timeline:

1791: a deposition from a Robert Wills was taken, stating that "Jane and George Gibson, dark mulattoes, who lived in the county of Charles City, and were free persons." He stated further about Jane Gibson who married Morris Evans, that she "practiced midwifery and doctoring." When asked if he knew any other "free mulattoes or blacks who have descended from a branch of the name Evans," Wills stated that he knew a number of them in Charles City: the Scott, Bradby, Smith, Redcross, Morris, and in Henrico the Bowman families, all who descended from Jane Evans the daughter of Jane Gibson" and that Jane was the ancestor of other "free mulattoes or blacks...some black, some nearly white and others dark mulattoes."

1792: Hannah Evans' son Thomas Gibson, alias Mingo Jackson, won his freedom with Robert Pleasants as his attorney.

1795: Hannah's other children won their freedom. Both cases were based on descent from a free woman.

1796: Amey Evans and her children and grandchildren petitioned for their freedom when their attorney issued a warrant on their slave owner David Allen to appear in Brunswick County District Court. The petition stated they were "lineally descended from a certain Frances Evans who lived and died a free woman...That the said Frances Evans having bound one of her daughters named Frances as an apprentice to a certain Lightfoot of New Kent County, the said Lightfoot did sell her as a slave and in consequence of the said sale the said Frances Evans and your petitioners her descendants have been detained in slavery, and are now detained in slavery by a certain David Allen of Mecklenburg County." One of the deponents for the trial stated that she "has often heard her husband say in his lifetime that Frances Evans was of Indian decent and from the complexion & strait black hair of Sarah Colley this deponent believes that they were descended from Indians."

1799: Amey Evans' Freedom suit abated in May 1799 by the death of slave owner David Allen.

1804: On 5 March 1804, newly-assigned court attorney Edmund Randolph filed a petition in the Superior Court of Chancery in Richmond for the freedom of the Evans family members still held in slavery to sue David Allen's executor Lewis Allen. It was submitted to the court that the Evans family were "children of a free woman of colour named Amey; who was the daughter of another free woman of colour named Sarah Colley, who was the daughter of another free woman of colour named Frances Evans; who was the daughter of another free woman of colour named Jane Gibson."

1809: On January 26, 1809, the deposition of executor Lewis Allen (of the David Allen estate) made a statement about one of Amey's sons: "a Negro man by the name Charles who ran away some eight or nine years since."

Unfortunately for Amey and her children, their attorney Edmund Randolph died in 1813, and their next attorney when the trial was held in Lynchburg City, Christopher Henderson Clark, had a stroke in 1820. The case was dismissed in 1821. Amey Evans and her descendants remained slaves for life until Emancipation.

Sadly, the line between freedom and slavery was razor thin.

Who are the descendants of the original Jews? Where are the descendants of the enslaved Hebrews who were brought to America? Today, with new technology available, many have been able to identify their ancestry and, in several cases, even identify their enslaved ancestors by means of modern genetic DNA testing. Also, we are able to understand a clearer picture of the history of human migrations due to DNA analysis and genetic sequencing.

This is also being used in trying to answer the question of: Who were the original Jews in Biblical times?

One such effort in that endeavor were the results of a DNA project in 2011, entitled "The History of African Gene Flow into Southern European, Levantines, and Jews." (Sources, Chapter 11) From this testing, it was discovered that people from Southern Europe, Palestine, Israel, Syria, and Jordan have inherited genetic material of Hamite origin. It was found that Syrian Jews, Iranian Jews, Iraqi Jews, Greek Jews, Turkish Jews, Italian Jews, and Ashkenazi Jews were detected with 3%-5% sub-Saharan African ancestry. These findings were explained as "evidence" regarding the "common origin" of those Jewish groups. The exact date of this Hamitic admixture was not determined, but it was estimated to have taken place between 1,600 and 3,400 years ago, or in other words, between the 15th Century BCE and the 5th Century CE. The researchers involved in that project went on to state that, although it was known the Mizrahi Iranian and Iraqi Jews had descended in part from the Jews who were exiled in Babylon in the 7th Century BCE, the researchers were amazed that they shared Hamitic admixture. The researchers concluded that the Jewish groups who participated descend from a "common ancestral population" which is "admixed with Africans," and "prior" to the Jewish Diaspora which occurred between the 8th and 6th Century BCE.

DNA technology is constantly improving. Case in point is the sequencing of Mummy DNA. Years ago it was considered impossible. Now, the successful genomic testing on ancient Egyptian mummies is happening. Recently, the DNA of a vizier to King Tuthmosis III of the 15th Century BCE, was sequenced, whose name was Rekhmire. The testing results revealed that Rekhmire was Nubian.

All this to say is that we are reminded again, DNA testing analysis can in many ways help to tell the story of the history of human migration and of the Jews when combined with historical facts. Welsh engraver Emanuel Bowen published a map of West Africa in 1747, describing the slave port Juda/Whydah by engraving the words, "Km of Juda or Whidah SLAVE COAST." A large population of black and Mulatto Jews began to appear in the 1780's in Suriname and Jamaica. Their descendants are now showing up on DNA genetic testings. Keep in mind that many who were enslaved during French Louisiana were sent to Suriname and Jamaica to work the French sugar cane plantations. And many of those enslaved in French Louisiana came from the slave market Juda in the Bight of Benin.

This journey first began by trying to trace both my mother's ancestors through her maternal line, the Lipscombs, and my paternal grandmother's ancestors, the Barnetts. The journey expanded by examining the family lines of four genetic cousins. This led to a discovery about colonial American history that was completely unknown to me. I thank all my cousins who corresponded and were open to exploring who our DNA ancestors were. Besides learning about James Ivey, a North Carolina landowner in 1773 who was the leader of a group of mulatto men squatting on the King's land, I found another document involving him in South Carolina. He had signed his name, along with others, on <u>a petition in 1794 to repeal</u> <u>a poll tax</u> on "all Free Negroes, Mustee, and Mulattos." In addition, a document was discovered involving a "George Ivie", who signed a petition along with others to the Council of Virginia <u>to repeal an</u> <u>Act in 1699</u> against English people in the colony "marrying with Negroes, Indians, or Mulattos." **Despite the ban on intermarriage, many Whites defied the law.**

Did this journey also help me discover that my paternal grand-mother's line – the Barnetts – were related to Charles Barnett, the FPOC of Albemarle County, Virginia? And, did I finally learn the truth about my maternal grandmother's ancestors – were they Hebrew Jews?

Before the answer to these questions are finally revealed, we must first answer the question raised at the beginning of this book about the two archaic prophecies that the ancient soothsayers recorded in the sacred text thousands of years ago regarding a coming Messiah who would restore the kingdom of Judah and bring peace – will these predictions really come true?

CHAPTER 12

The Hebrew Scrolls Foretold the Coming Mashiach In 1st Century

There is nothing more important, more urgent, more purposeful, than to embrace and understand the progressive out-workings of the Most High Yahuah's expressed will and purpose. One major way this can be demonstrated is by understanding the many prophecies recorded in the Tanakh, the Hebrew Scriptures, especially those in the Ketuvim, that shed more knowledge on the prophecy in Eden regarding the coming Seed of Judah, Ha-Mashiach (the Messiah).

One of the writings in the Ketuvim that has revealed key essential understanding about Ha-Mashiach is the prophetic Book of Daniel, which describe *three* major "Comings" of the Messiah, whom every person on earth now living at this very hour need to know and act upon.

The following texts will cover the Messiah's first Coming. In Chapter 16 will reveal his Second Coming, or *Parousia*. The events that will occur during his third "Coming" will be covered in the final chapter.

At Daniel 9:20-23, we read Daniel describing how the angel Gabriel came to him to deliver a vision about the coming Messiah:

"While I was still speaking and praying and confessing my sin and the sin of my people Israel and making my request for favor before Yahuah my God concerning the holy mountain of my God, yes, while I was yet speaking in prayer, the man Gabriel, whom I had previously seen in the vision, came to me when I was extremely weary at about the time of the evening gift offering.

And he gave me understanding, saying: "O Daniel, now I have come to give you insight and understanding. When you began your entreaty the word went out, and I have come to report it to you, because you are someone very precious. So consider the matter and understand the vision."

The vision Gabriel gave to Daniel is stated in Daniel 9:24-27. Let us now breakdown its key points:

Daniel 9:24: "**Seventy weeks** are decreed upon thy people and upon thy holy city, to make an end of sin, and to forgive iniquity, and to bring in everlasting righteousness, and to seal vision and prophet, and to anoint the Holy of Holies."

We notice a time period of *Seventy weeks* is decreed upon Daniel's people, the Hebrew Jews. What is the purpose of the time period? "To make an end of sin, and to forgive iniquity, and to bring in everlasting righteousness." Similar to how the Most High had decreed *70 years* upon His people to be in captivity to Babylon, and then *after those years had expired* the Jews were then released from Babylon's bondage, *so too, after Seventy weeks*, there would be *an end of their sins and everlasting righteousness would be brought in.*

"And to seal vision and prophet." In other words, the fulfillment of Daniel's vision concerning the Messiah would confirm all of the Most High's promises and prophecies.

Was the Seventy weeks in this vision to be understood as meaning *literal* weeks? Let us continue.

Daniel 9:25: "From the going forth of the word to restore and to build Jerusalem until Messiah, there will be seven weeks, also sixty-two weeks. Jerusalem will return and be actually rebuilt, with a public square and moat, but in the straits of the times."

"From the going forth of the word to restore and to build Jerusalem." This part of the vision was fulfilled in the 20th year of King Artaxerxes of Persia, when the king gave Nehemiah permission to *restore and to build Jerusalem*, as recorded in Nehemiah 2: 1-8. The 20th year of King Artaxerxes was in 455 BCE, and upon his arrival, Nehemiah began rebuilding the walls of Jerusalem between the months of Ab and Elul of that year (Nehemiah 2:17-20; 6:15). The Jewish months of Ab and Elul correspond to July/August, and August/September. We recall that Jerusalem, and the temple, had been destroyed by Nebuchadnezzar of Babylon in 607 BCE. Some of the Jews had returned to Jerusalem with Zerubbabel in 537 BCE to begin rebuilding. But the work was not completed.

"There will be seven weeks." This is referring to the time period of completing the restoration of the city Jerusalem.

"Also sixty-two weeks." This is relating to the time period *after* the completion of the city until the coming of the Messiah.

So according to the vision given to Daniel, the Seventy weeks were divided into three periods: (1) seven weeks, (2) sixty-two weeks, and (3) one week, all adding up to "Seventy weeks."

Was Jerusalem and the temple rebuilt in seven literal weeks? No. It took about twenty-one years alone just to complete the temple (Ezra 3:8-10; Ezra 6:13-15). So this vision is not referring to literal weeks, it is referring to prophetic weeks. The angel Gabriel did not mention days in the vision, so these are not weeks of seven days each. *These are weeks of years.* The Most High put the vision in prophetic code. *Each week is seven years long.* Notice Daniel 9:24 in the *American Translation* and the *Revised English Bible*:

> "Seventy weeks of years are destined for your people and for your holy city."

> "Seventy times seven years are marked out for your people and your holy city."

So the "Seventy weeks" mean prophetic years. When do they begin? Daniel 9:25 stated: "From the going forth of the word to restore and to build Jerusalem." Thus, the Seventy weeks began in the year 455 BCE during the 20th year of King Artaxerxes of Persia, when Nehemiah began rebuilding the walls of Jerusalem, between the months of Ab and Elul of that year. The "seven weeks, also sixty-two weeks" is prophetic of *483 years*. Therefore, counting 483 years from 455 BCE would end in the year of 29 CE.

Daniel 9:26: "And after the sixty-two weeks, Messiah will be cut off, with nothing for himself. And the people of a leader that is coming will destroy the city and the holy place."

This text reveals that the "holy place" – the temple – would be destroyed again. However, the Messiah will be "cut off" – he will die – *before* the destruction of the second temple.

Daniel 9:27: "And he must keep the covenant in force for the many for one week; and at the half of the week he will cause sacrifice and gift offering to cease."

We will discuss the key points of this text shortly. But beforehand, let us examine further the "seven weeks, also sixty-two weeks" that make up the prophetic code of 483 years, which started in 455 BCE during the months Ab-Elul and end in 29 CE.

In one of the books of the Gospels – the Book of Luke – written between 56-58 CE in Greek by a physician, recorded this:

"In the 15th year of the reign of Tiberius Caesar, when Pontius Pilate was governor of Jude, Herod was district ruler of Galilee, Philip his brother was district ruler of the country of Ituraea and Trachonitis, and Lysanias was district ruler of Abilene, in the days of chief priest Annas and of Caiaphas, God's declaration came to John the son of Zechariah in the wilderness…Now the people were in expectation and all of them were reasoning in their hearts about John, "May he perhaps be the Christ?" (Luke 3:1, 15)

The people in Palestine at that time were in expectation of *the Christ*, which is the Greek word for *Messiah* in Hebrew. So in effect, the people were reasoning, "May he perhaps be the Messiah?" The people knew for years the prophecy of Daniel about the Seventy weeks, so that is why they were in expectation. They knew the time for the appearance of the Messiah was approaching near. Many thought that perhaps John the baptist was the "Anointed One." However, there is something else in this text passage that must not be missed.

The writer and physician Luke stated that these events were happening, "In the 15th year of the reign of Tiberius Caesar."

Tiberius Caesar was named Roman Emperor by the Roman Senate in September 14 CE, after Gaius Octavius, or better known as Caesar Augustus, died on August 19, 14 CE. This is all confirmed by ancient historian Suetonius, as well as the official Roman Fasti (Calendar). (See Sources, Chapter 12) Why is this important? The writer Luke continues:

"John gave the answer, saying to all: "I, for my part, baptize you with water, but the one stronger than I am is coming, the lace of whose sandals I am not worthy to untie. He will baptize you with holy spirit and with fire...Now when all the people were baptized, Yeshua too was baptized.""

Luke reports that John baptized a person named Yeshua/Yahshua the Baptist, in the 15th year of the reign of Tiberius Caesar. Another writer, Matthew, who was a tax collector, wrote an account in 40 CE of this same event, which also became part of the gospels:

"In those days John the Baptist came preaching in the wilderness of Judea...Then Yeshua came from Galilee to the Jordan to John, in order to be baptized by him...after being baptized, Yeshua immediately came up from the water." (Matthew 3:1,13,16)

Regarding Yeshua/Yahshua, both accounts by Luke and Matthew stated that his parents were Joseph and Mary of Nazareth, who were both members of the tribe of Judah, and both descendants of King David, according to the Jewish genealogical rolls that were available at that time. (See Notes) So what was the 15th year of Tiberius Caesar's reign? Since the Roman Senate confirmed him in September 14 CE, his 15th year would have been around September, 29 CE.

According to the vision given to Daniel, Ha-Mashiach would appear when the "seven weeks, also sixty-two weeks" ended, which began counting for 483 years starting in 455 BCE around the months of Ab/Elul when Nehemiah completed the walls of Jerusalem, and thus, would end in the year of 29 CE.

Yeshua was baptized in the autumn of 29 CE, in the 15th year of the reign of Tiberius Caesar.

Coincidence?

The Most High said that there will be those "Who have eyes but do not see, and ears but do not hear." (Isaiah 6:9,10)

Let us examine the last part of Daniel's vision:

Daniel 9:27: "And he must keep the covenant in force for the many for one week; and at the half of the week he will cause sacrifice and gift offering to cease."

Here we come down to the last week of the vision, the "one week", which, when added to the other weeks, makes the "Seventy weeks" in total. As has already been established, these are prophetic weeks. So, to be consistent, in this prophecy the "one week" is actually, not seven days, but are *7 years*. And, the vision states that "He" the Messiah, "will cause sacrifice and gift offering to cease" *at the half of the week."* Let us examine this final part of the vision in relation to Yeshua, the one who was baptized in the Jordan River in the autumn of 29 CE.

At Luke 4, verses 1 and 2, it states that after Yeshua was baptized he went to the wilderness for 40 days. This would have been September going into October 29 CE.

Using another book of the gospels as a historical reference point, the account of the fisherman John, let us see what it reveals how many times Yeshua attended the annual Passover in Jerusalem. The Passover was celebrated annually on Nisan 14 after sundown.

John 2:13: "Now the Passover of the Jews was near, and Yeshua went up to Jerusalem" This was Passover of 30 CE.

John 5:1: "After this there was a festival of the Jews, and Yeshua went up to Jerusalem." This was Passover of 31 CE

John 6:3,4: "So Yeshua went up on a mountain and sat down there with his disciples. Now the Passover, the festival of the Jews, was near." This was Passover 32 CE

John 12:1: "Six days before the Passover, Yeshua arrived at Bethany."

John 13:2: "Now because he knew before the festival of the Passover that his hour had come for him to leave this world and go to the Father…the evening meal was going on." This was the evening of Passover 33 CE.

In 33 CE, that date would have corresponded to our April 14th. The months of the Jews generally ran from the middle of the month to the middle of the next month. If one examines the Passovers that Yeshua attended according to the accounts in the Book of John, we notice that Yeshua attended the annual Passover between a period of three years and six months:

1 year: The autumn of 29 CE to October 30 CE

2nd year: The autumn of 30 CE to October 31 CE
3rd year: The autumn of 31 CE to October 32 CE

Six Months: October 32, November 32, December 32, January 33, February 33, and then the sixth month, March, which ran from mid-March to mid April 33 CE.

Daniel 9:27: "And he must keep the covenant in force for the many for one week; and *at the half of the week* he will cause sacrifice and gift offering to cease." The prophetic "half of the week" meant 3 years and six months.

Yahshua/Yeshua was hung on a stake (not a cross) on Passover, Nisan 14, 33 CE

Coincidence?

According to the Gospel accounts, Yahshua/Yeshua stated on many occasions that he was the son of the Most High, and was sent by Him to give his life as a guilt offering for many and to carry the sins of the people. (See Isaiah 53) Was he the foretold Coming Seed of Judah?

What other ancient historical sources, outside biblical texts, mention the events of Yeshua's life?

CHAPTER 13

Historical Evidentiary Supports Yeshua/ Yahshua Is Foretold Messiah

Here are historical sources, outside the Bible, which speak of a man known as Jesus Christ as a historical person whom people in the 1st Century CE either saw, spoke to, referenced, or heard verifiable reports about.

Spoiler: These are strong evidentiary sources. You be the Judge.

- "When, therefore, Ananus was of this disposition, he thought he had now a proper opportunity…so he convened the judges of the Sanhedrin and brought before them a man named James, *the brother of Jesus who was called the Christ*, and certain others." Josephus, *Antiquities of the Jews*, Book 20, Chapter 9

- "Chritus, the founder of the name, had undergone the death penalty in the reign of Tiberius, by sentence of the procurator Pontius Pilate, and the pernicious superstition was checked for a moment, only to break out once more, not only in Judaea, the first source of the evil, but even in Rome." Tacitus, *Annals*, Book 15, Chapter 44. Written circa 116 CE. (Chritus was the Latin word for Christ)

- *"On the eve of Passover Yeshu the Nazarene was hanged."*
  Gemara, Babylonia Talmud, Sanhedrin 43a, Munich
  Codex. The oldest known complete manuscript of the
  Babylonian Talmud. The Munich Codex is also known as
  Hebrew Manuscript 95. 9th Century CE. (Yeshu was the
  Aramaic word for Yeshua)

- "And the women also, which came with him from Galilee,
  followed after, and beheld the sepulchre, and how his
  body was laid. And they returned, and prepared spices
  and ointments...Now upon the first day of the week, very
  early in the morning, they came...bringing the spices they
  had prepared...And they entered in, and found not the
  body of the Lord Jesus. And it came to pass, as they were
  much perplexed thereabout, behold, two men stood by
  them in shining garments...He is not here, but is risen...
  And returned from the sepulchre, and told all these
  things unto the eleven, and to all the rest. It was Mary
  Magdalene, and Joanna, and Mary the mother of James,
  and other women that had been with them, which told
  these things unto the apostles. *And their words seemed
  to them as idle tales, and they believed them not."* (Luke
  23:55-24:1-11) According to the Bible, it was the women
  who were the first to learn that Yeshua had risen from
  the dead. In ancient Palestine, women were looked down
  upon. The testimony of a woman was considered equal to
  that of a slave. It is no surprise, then, that the apostles did
  not believe the women, in view of the prevailing attitude
  toward women at that time. Being imperfect, the apostles
  still had things to work on. Today, many believe the

Greek Scriptures of the Bible were invented. So then, why would Luke record that women first discovered Yeshua's resurrection if this really did not happen? Why would these details be invented back then, which would portray the men in an unfavorable and embarrassing light if it did not happen? The account only makes sense if it was true.

- In Justin Martyr's work *Dialogue with Trypho,* written between 155-160 CE, he mentions that certain Jews were saying that *the body of Jesus was stolen from the tomb by his disciples.* There is no contemporary written record found anywhere that refuted Martyr's statement. It was a common belief, which he was merely echoing at the time. *But this statement could not have been said if the tomb was __not__ empty. If it were common knowledge that Jesus' body was still in the tomb, then why would a belief that the body was stolen still persist?* Martyr would have been making himself look foolish! So the tomb *was* empty. *Yeshua's body was not there.* Chapter 108

- According to official Roman governor reports written by Pontius Pilate, he stated that Yeshua was nailed in both his hands and feet, *and had performed miracles to heal diseases and raise the dead. The Acts of Pontius Pilate,* mentioned in *First Apology of Justin Martyr,* Chapters 35 & 48. Written between 155-157 CE.

(See Sources, Chapter 13)

CHAPTER 14

Why Did the Papacy of Christendom Conspire to Enslave *Africa?*

Did the Holy Roman Papacy attack and kidnap people in Africa because the people were African? Or was there another reason why they started the Trans-Atlantic Slave Trade?

We already know that Hebrews have lived in Africa for millenniums. The Twelve Tribes of Israel were formed in Egypt. Hebrews and Egyptians (The term Egyptian includes Nubians and Cushites) intermarried during Jacob's residence there with his twelve sons. King David acquired gold from West Africa and from Carthage, North Africa. (See the Book *"The Line of Shem and the Seed of Judah"*). Hebrew Israelites were sent by the Assyrians to Kush as slaves in 740 BCE. We also know that many Hebrews moved to Egypt to start colonies, such as in Elephantine and Alexandria. In 607 BCE, when the Babylonians took the Kingdom of Judah as slaves, a sizable group of Judean Israelites escaped to Tahpanes, Egypt. Also, many Hebrews in Africa would journey to Jerusalem annually to celebrate the Passover at the temple, and then return to Africa. In the year 70, history recounts the destruction of Jerusalem and its temple by the Roman armies, and Hebrew Jews were scattered to North Africa and other parts of the Roman Empire, while 97,000 Jews were sold into slavery. Yeshua had said, "Jerusalem will be trampled on by the

Gentiles until the times of the Gentiles are fulfilled." After the second Jewish revolt between 132-135, the Jews were scattered, killed, and sold again into slavery, and the Romans banned them from entering the city of Jerusalem for nearly two centuries. The province of Judea was renamed *Syria Palaestina* in an attempt to get rid of the name Judea. The Hebrews who believed that Yeshua was the Messiah were also scattered.

So with this backdrop of millions of Hebrew Jews already living in Africa by the 1st Century, the question can be asked again: **Did the Holy Roman Papacy attack and capture people in Africa because the people were African? Or was there another reason why they started the Trans-Atlantic Slave Trade?**

The answer is, the Papacy focused on the continent of Africa for two reasons. One reason was because they wanted to enslave African peoples whom they viewed as savage, pagan, non-Christian. The other reason can be easily explained by answering this simple question: Did the Holy Roman Church of Christendom view Jews as friends or enemies? Consider the following evidence.

In 325, Roman Emperor Constantine the Great presided over the Council of Nicaea, a convening of "apostate Christian" bishops in all the realm of Christendom, in order to reach consensus on various apostate church doctrine and man-made traditions of ritual law. At the end of the council, it had been decided that Rome should not celebrate their festival of Easter on the same date as the Jewish Passover because:

> "...it appeared an unworthy thing that in the celebration of this most holy feast we should follow the practice of the Jews."

Constantine himself expresses the decision this way:

> "It was, in the first place, declared improper to follow the custom of the Jews in the celebration of this holy festival, because, their hands having been stained with crime...Let us, then have nothing in common with the Jews, who are our adversaries...avoiding all contact with that evil way"

In 329, Constantine issued laws prohibiting Jews to own "Christian" slaves; Conversion of "Christians" to Judaism to be punishable by death; and forbidding Jews to perform circumcision on slaves. Another law was passed prohibiting marriages between Jews and "Christians."

By 411, the Germanic tribe of the Visigoths of Gaul moved into Iberia, a Roman province, and took possession of it. This Roman province, originally called *Hispania Ulterior*, was a place for retired military who had fought for Rome, starting with Augustus. Emperor Marcus Salvius Otho was once the governor of this province in 58/59 BCE. The province had a golden statue of Emperor Titus who, as general during the Jewish revolt in 70 CE, had sent 97,000 Hebrew Jews into slavery. Some of those slaves may have been sent to the province of Hispania.

The Visigoths ruled Iberia for the next 300 years. Some Jews, who had already scattered to Iberia or migrated there from Syria Palestine prior, would soon face severe edicts. Between 589-694, several edicts against Jews were passed by the Visigoth's Council of Toledo:

> 589 CE – Forced baptism on children of mixed Jewish/ Catholic marriages; Forbidden to hold public office.

613 CE – Jews to be expelled or convert to the Catholic Church; As many as 90,000 converted; Some fled to North Africa and intermingled with the Berber tribes, converting many of them and intermarriage.

633 CE – Catholics practicing Judaism secretly are to have their children taken away from them.

653 CE – Forbidden to worship; Anyone discovered to have aided Jews in their worship shall face seizure of one fourth of their property and excommunication.

694 CE – Visigoth King Egica learned of an alleged plot between Jews in Iberia and Hebrews in North Africa who were collaborating with the Moors for an invasion; The Visigoth king declared all Jews to be made slaves and their masters to insure their slaves not observe Jewish customs. These measures were only partly implemented.

Do we see a pattern of behavior by the Holy Roman Papacy and her Rome-European allies towards Jews? How did the Papacy view the Jews? They hated them. The Jews were considered the "Enemies of Christ" (Their version of Christ, not the true Christ Messiah Yahshua/Yeshua). As previously mentioned, millions of Hebrew Jews were living in Africa by the 1st Century. So if the Roman Papacy had declared a war on the "Enemies of Christendom," how far would they travel, do you think, in order to "Capture" and "Convert" these enemies?

On April 30, 711 CE, an army of 7000 Berbers under the Moor Tariq ibn Ziyad landed at Gibraltar, followed by Arab Muslim soldiers, which led to eventual Muslim rule of Southern Iberia. The persecution of Jews under the Visigoths now ended with the Moor/Arab conquest. In 1095, the Papacy proclaimed the Crusades on Muslims, in response to Muslim control of Jerusalem. These Crusades lasted from 1095-1291.

Conspiring first with Portugal, and later with Spain, the Papacy of the Holy Roman Empire of Christendom schemed a plan: "With due meditation" the Papacy would "by letters of ours" grant King Afonso V of Portugal to capture "Guineamen *and other Negroes* taken by force *and subdue all" Enemies of Christendom,* and "to reduce them to perpetual slavery." Who did they view as the enemies of Christendom? *All Hebrew Jews, as well as all the followers of Yeshua/ Yahshua, those who belonged to "The Way."*

This was why Christendom invaded Africa. Starting from 1441, a blitzkrieg to colonize Hebrew West Africa was now underway. The Papacy actually followed the same route that the once mighty military power Carthage took when it sent out Hanno the Navigator, who accomplished a circumnavigation of Northwest Africa in the 5th Century BC. Hanno and his fleet of sixty ships set sail from Cadiz, Carthage (now part of Spain) and founded colonies in the West coast, such as Cerne, Bay of Arguin, Senegal, Cape Verde, and Gambia. Some say he also reached Cameroon (See the book *The Line of Shem & the Seed of Judah*). This voyage was also to explore the gold routes from West Africa to Carthage.

Thus, the Holy Roman Church of the Papacy had Portugal and Spain follow these same routes, resulting in slave raids and slave ports being set up from Arguin Bay to Senegal between 1443-1455. In addition, the Papacy was also interested in securing gold and other wealth in West Africa, just as she proved when landing in the Americas in 1492: searching for gold and turning the local Indigenous into slaves. The Papacy's goal in West Africa would be no different.

Here is the entire edict, or papal bull, of January 8, 1455:

"And so it came to pass that when a number of ships of this kind had explored and taken possession of very many harbors, islands, and seas, that at length came to **the province of Guinea**, and having taken possession of some islands and harbors and the sea adjacent to that province, sailing father they came <u>to the mouth of a certain great river</u> commonly supposed to be the Nile, **and war was waged for some years against the peoples of those parts** in the name of the said King Alfonso…Thence also many Guineamen **and other Negroes, taken by force**, and some by barter of unprohibited articles, or by other lawful contract of purchase, have been sent to the said kingdoms…**We** weighing all and singular the premises with due meditation, and noting that since we had formerly by other letters of ours granted among other things free and ample faculty to the aforesaid King Alfonso — **to invade, search out, capture, vanquish, and subdue all Saracens** and pagans whatsoever, *and other enemies of Christ wheresoever placed*, and the kingdoms, dukedoms, principalities, dominions, possessions, and all movable and immovable goods whatsoever held and possessed by them and to reduce their persons to *perpetual slavery*, and to apply and appropriate to himself and his successors the kingdoms, dukedoms, counties, principalities, dominions, possessions, and goods, *and to convert them to his and their use and profit…*"

This was during the mid-1400's in Africa. The expulsion of the Jews in 1492 and the subsequent hunting and capturing of them hadn't even come about yet. That would be some forty years later. Notice in this papal bull, it stated how the slave traders arrived at "the mouth of a certain river." This was the Senegal River, which some called the "Western Nile" at that time. The *Saracens* were also singled out for capture, which was another term for "Arabs," who actually were Hebrews too, through Abraham's lines with Hagar and Keturah (but not from the Hebrew line of Jacob – the Israelites).

By the backing and power handed from the Papacy, another slave-trading post was set up, called *El Mina* in 1482. Ten years later, the Alhambra Decree was passed in Catholic Spain, giving the Jews four months, July 31, to either convert to the Catholic Church or be expelled. The exact number expelled is unknown, as some estimate 40,000, while others estimate 100,000 Jews. Many fled to Africa, while others to the Ottoman Empire and Italy. But the worst was not over. The Papacy issued two papal bulls on May 3, 1493, granting Spain the same permissions and favors in West Africa as did Portugal. King Ferdinand sent instructions to his colonial governor in Haiti:

> "Because with great care we have procured the conversion of the Indians to our Holy Catholic Faith, and furthermore, if there are still people there who are doubtful of the faith in their own conversions, it would be a hindrance, and therefore we will not permit, nor allow to go there Moors, nor Jews nor heretics nor reconciled heretics, nor persons who are recently converted to our faith, **except if they are negro slaves,** or other slaves, that have been born under the dominion of our natural Christian subjects." (September 16, 1501)

In other words, no free Moors or free Jews would be sent to Haiti; except if they are *Negro slaves*. So again, the reasons for the Holy Roman Papacy invading Africa was not only to convert and enslave the Africans peoples with all their diverse cultures and rich knowledge, but also because the Papacy wanted to capture and convert the "Enemies of Christendom," who were Hebrew Jews, as well as the followers of Yeshua/Yahshua.

Just as slavery was forecast in Deuteronomy 28, notice how it was foretold also by the Most High through John, a disciple and Apostle of Yeshua, in Revelation chapter 18:

> *"One of the seven angels who had the seven bowls came and said to me: Come, I will show you the judgment on the great prostitute who sits on many waters...**Babylon the Great**...a full cargo of gold, silver, precious stones, pearls...cattle, sheep, horses, carriages, **slaves, and human beings...and every ship captain and every man that voyages anywhere, and sailors and all those who make a living by the sea, stood at a distance"***

Is there evidence that Hebrew Jews were sent to America as slaves?

CHAPTER 15

Hebrew Jews: Trans-Atlantic Slave Trade to America

The Portuguese Crown began meddling with the Kingdom of *Kongo* and the region of west-central Congo around 1483 CE. At first, it was for the purposes of exchanging cultures and trade. Even nobles from the royal court of Kongo and Catholic missionaries from Portugal were exchanged between both kingdoms by 1491. Within the region of the Congo lived nomadic Jews, many who had been pushed out of Egypt-Nubia due to the Muslim conquest of Egypt that had occurred in the 7th Century CE. These "wandering Jews" moved into the Congo to avoid persecution and forced conversion to Islam from the Muslims.

In 1575, the Portuguese had established a colony called Portuguese Angola, along the West African coastline, which became slave ports. Oddly enough, it was during this same time when the Italian cosmographer from Venice, Livio Sanuto, was drawing maps of Africa he hoped to publish for the world to see. On one of his maps of Africa, Sanuto wrote in Latin, *Iudeorum Terra*, when translated means "Land of the Jews." Where in Africa was this land? Sanuto later died in 1576, and his brother Giulio Sanuto eventually published, in 1588, twelve maps of Africa that Livio had completed.

This historical information needs to be fully understood and linked to the context of the Trans-Atlantic Slave trade. The majority of enslaved who were brought against their will to Colonial Virginia, the Carolinas, other parts of the South, and Colonial New York were from the Congo region.

Where specifically in Africa was the "Land of The Jews" that Sanuto discovered and appears on his map, dated 1588? **It existed on the borders of the Kongo Kingdom by the Nile River.** Who were these Jews? Did they become victims of the Trans-Atlantic Slave Trade? To answer these questions, we must examine the history of the Kingdom of Abyssinia (Ethiopia).

The Kingdom of Abyssinia traces the beginning of its early history with the Kingdom of Axum, who had taken over the Kingdom of Kush when it declined in power. (See the book *Three Brothers – 1626, the Genealogy of the World*) The first king to rule Axum was King Ezana (320-360 ce), who embraced apostatized Christianity. How did this happen? Ezana was influenced by Frumentius, the first bishop of Axum and follower of Roman Emperor Constantine's religion – an apostatized version of Christianity called Roman Catholicism. Before becoming appointed bishop, Frumentius, a missionary and former slave servant in Axum's kingdom, had requested Athanasius the Pope of Alexandria (who laid the groundwork for the Trinity doctrine heresy) to send a bishop and priests to Axum. Athanasius chose instead to appoint Frumentius as bishop of Axum. Frumentius converted and baptized King Ezana, who then made Constantine the Great's apostatized Christianity the official State religion of Axum, calling it the Coptic Orthodox Church.

The Abyssinian, or Ethiopian Empire began in 1270 with the establishment of the Solomonic dynasty by their first king, Yekuno Amlak. The empire also affirmed the continuation of the Coptic Orthodox

Church, later the Ethiopian Orthodox Church. The Solomonic dynasty, according to tradition contained in the *Kebra Negast*, is based on the belief of the Ethiopian Orthodox Church that King Solomon of Israel and the Queen of Sheba had a son named Menilek, (considered the first Solomonic Emperor) who allegedly brought the Ark of the Covenant to Ethiopia, and therefore all the kings of Ethiopia are viewed as descending from Solomon, king of Israel.

However, on the border of Abyssinia and the Nile River, not far from Gondar, lay a group of people who considered themselves Israelites and lived in the mountains near the Nile between Khartoum and Gondar. The author John Ogilby in his 1670 book, *Africa an Accurate Description*, called this group "The Country of the Jews, or Kingdom of Semen", and described their location this way: "It lieth enclosed with Mountains and Deserts, on the East extending themselves to Nile; on the South to Congo, and the Equinoctial Line; in the West to the Kingdom of Benin; and on the North over against Davine and Medra, a Country but little known, and less conversed with, and under the Dominion of the Abyssines."

The origin of those Jews are still unknown to this day. Some say they were driven from Judea when Jerusalem was destroyed. Others say they originated from the Himyarites in Yemen. Oral history in Ethiopia today say they were once called the *Falasha* (Exile). Others say they were from the tribe of Dan. But whatever their Hebrew origin was, one thing is for sure – they were hated by the Emperors of Abyssinia and hunted down. As early as 1255 (and probably earlier), war campaigns were waged against them, starting with Abyssinian King Icon-Amlac of Shoa, who attacked the kings of "Semen," or "Samen," because they did not pay tributes to the Emperor.

Several more Abyssinian kings continued their assault on the *Falasha*, or Beta Israel:

King Amda Seyon I – (Emperor from 1314 to 1344), in 1329 he led a campaign on the "Land of the Jews" in the Northern provinces, where many Beta Israel were gaining prominence.

King Yeshaq I – (Emperor from 1414 to 1429), led a warring campaign against rebelling Beta Israel areas, nineteen miles North of Gondar. Yeshaq's purpose was to force Beta Israel to convert to the Coptic Ethiopian Orthodox Church or lose their land.

King Zara Yaqob – (Emperor from 1434 to 1468), led a campaign in the North against the Falasha (Beta Israel), and the Agaw, who were described as a "Hebrewic Religion." The Agaw spoke a Cushite language (part of the Afro-Asiatic Languages) and spoke other subdivision languages, which formed the main sub stratum influence on Ethiopian Semitic languages.

(In 1507, Portugal sent their envoy Matthews to Abyssinia to ask for aid against the Adal Sultanate and the Ottoman Empire for control of the trade route to India, via the Red Sea. A Portuguese Mission was established in 1520. Conversion was the goal).

King Malak Sagad I – (born as Sarsa Dengel, Emperor from 1563 to 1597), departed from Tigray in 1580 to conduct a war campaign against "the Falasha King of Samen" in Semen province which possessed great inaccessible mountains. At that same time, other provinces under his reign were being attacked by separate army forces. Despite being notified of these developments, Malak declined to defend his other provinces and instead focused on Beta Israel, saying: "It is better for me that I fight with enemies of the blood of Jesus Christ than go fight against the Galla." By saying "enemies" he meant Jews.

(Early historian Leo Africanus said of this fortified army of Jews, "A most populous nation of the Jewish stock under a mighty King, where they call the Land of the Hebrews…on the North the Kingdom of Goiame, there are certain mountains, peopled with Jews." (See Sources, Chapter 15)

King Susenyos I – (Emperor from 1607 to 1632), according to traveler James Bruce, while on a visit there in the 18th Century, was given access to Ethiopian records, and wrote about King Susenyos, "In the year 1617, [two years before 1619, author's insert] without assigning any reason for the treacherous act, Su[se]n[yo]s sent armed forces to massacre all the Jews **wherever they could be found**, and in this general holocaust, Gideon the King perished, and with him the Jewish Kingdom of Samen." In the book *Jews of Africa* (1920, by Sidney Mendelssohn), pgs 19,20, Mendelssohn makes a powerful point by saying King Susenyos unwisely calculated that he had "extinguished, by one blow, the religion" which existed in Ethiopia "long before Christianity" by the "butchery" he had inflicted. He goes on to say, "the survivors merely dispersed to adjoining territories" and more than likely "lived as secret Jews" after they were later forced to accept an apostatized "rite of baptism." During his reign, King Susenyos converted to Catholicism in 1624, resulting in uprisings, civil unrest, and deaths in his kingdom. He eventually abdicated his throne to his son Fasilides.

King Fasilides – (Emperor from 1632 to 1667), he continued the attacks on the Agaw and Beta Israel that his father Susenyos had begun.

Another ethnic group that garnered the wrath of Abyssinia were the Shanqella – a dark-skinned nilotic people who also lived in the region of "The Land of the Hebrews" near South Sudan. They were regarded by the Abyssinians as slave reserves. For example, Emperor Iyasu I (ruled 1682 to 1706) took many of them as slaves, males & females, from the Shanqella towns of Gisa and Gorsi. The Shanqella are also documented as Shanqilla, and Shankella. The League of Nations released a report in 1935, detailing the dehumanization of this exonym group under the Ethiopian Empire. **The term Shanqella is thought to have derived from the Agaw substratum.**

What was the policy of Slavery in Ethiopia, and did their enslaved become a part of the Trans-Atlantic Slave Trade? The Abyssinia Emperor Gelawdewos, in February 1548, passed an edict banning the sale of Ethiopian "Christians" to be exported abroad. His intention was not to end the slave trade completely. Captives could be sold if they were non-Christian, which applied also to Hebrew Jews, if they were not Orthodox Christian. (References to the paragraphs about Ethiopia, see Sources, Chapter 15)

Some nearby slave markets were the Kingdom of Kaffa in the Ethiopian highlands, the Kingdom of Kongo markets, and Luanda in Portuguese Angola. Ethiopia also sold the enslaved to markets in Arabia. Portuguese traders also acquired slaves captured from Ethiopia through intermediaries in neighboring areas, who traded them to the Portuguese. As was noted earlier, the Portuguese eventually no longer relied on Kongo alone to provide them with slaves, but instead went directly to Kongo's partners to supply their demand.

Is there documented evidence that Hebrew Jews in West Africa were enslaved and brought to America? Yes. Let us consider the Ewe, Bambara, and the Igbo (Ebo) peoples. Then we will look at the forced conversion of Jews to Islam, the Arabic language that American slaves spoke, and finally, the Gullah people of Georgia/South Carolina. (For more evidence of Hebrew Jews brought to America, see the author's previous book, *The Line of Shem and the Seed of Judah*).

The Ewe, or Eve people of Ghana, Benin, and Togo were discussed earlier in Chapter 3 (Ewe and Eve is pronounced "Eh-way" and "Eh-vay"). By the 13th Century, they had migrated to Ketu village in the Oyo Empire (Yoruba-Nigeria) from the Sudan/Kongo region according to their oral history, and observed several Hebrew Israelite customs. But between 1519 and 1865, millions of Akan, Fon, Ga, and Ewe people were enslaved and exported through the Trans-Atlantic Slave Trade from the Bight of Benin, which was part of what was called "the Slave Coast." The Bight of Benin was a long stretch of coastal land with several slave ports stretching from Nigeria to Ghana (Ghana, or Gold Coast, had its own slave ports stretching to the Windward Coast with its ports, then stretching to ports in the Pepper Coast of Liberia, and then to ports in Sierra Leone, and Senegal-Gambia).

From 1519 to 1800, the Bight of Benin shipped about 2 million enslaved persons, out of which at least 1 million – one half – were shipped from the port called *Juda*, or Ouidah (also called Whydah). The Portuguese traders called the port *Ajuda*, because **"its inhabitants were said to be Jews"** and **"considered to be a remnant of scattered tribes of Israel."**

In fact, Juda/Ouidah was one of the largest slave ports in West Africa. Hebrew Israelites in the region speaking Arabic called it YAHOODA. Ewe, Fon, and Akan were shipped to Brazil, Haiti,

Suriname, Trinidad, the French West Indies, and Colonial Louisiana to work the French West Indies, and Colonial Louisiana to work the French sugar plantations. In early 19th Century Brazil, the Ewe, along with Fon, Mahi, & Allada, began to be called the *Jeje*, whereas those who were enslaved from Oyo, Ilorin, Ketu, and Yoruba were called the *Najos*. Thus, the Ewe in Brazil came to be known as the *Jeje Ewe*. In Salvador, Brazil in 1835, there was a population of over 2,600 enslaved Jeje in that region. In 1848, there were ten Jeje who were free persons in Santana Parish, Brazil. Another development in Brazil was a religion that formed during the 19th Century called Jeje, which was a mixture of West African traditional beliefs and Catholicisim. Today there is hardly any trace left of Hebrew Judaism being practiced among the Ewe people, except for a small percentage in Benin. (Sources, Chapter 15)

In 1817, map engraver Thomas Bowdich drew a map of West Africa while stationed there by the British. He produced his map, incidently, the same year as the slave rebellion of 1817 in the Oyo Empire of Nigeria, as a Muslim slave uprising erupted at Ilorin that severely weakened Oyo's control over its region, which later led to Oyo's collapse in a civil war. However, notated on Bowdich's map was a region and a people called *Bambara*, not far from Mali (See map). Who were they?

Appearing in a North Carolina newspaper in 1853, the Carolina Weekly carried a shocking article to its Southern readers, entitled: *Negro Jews*. The article went on to say that a missionary in West Africa had been given a report from a German traveler that there were a large number of Negro Jews called *Bambara* who practice Judaism and hold a copy of the Hebrew Pentateuch.

The Bambara, who struggled to keep their identity by resisting conversion to Islam, were captured and taken by slave traders to the slave market at Juda. The French ship *Aurore* arrived at Juda on August 28, 1718. *Aurore* then headed out on a six-month voyage, arriving at Dauphin Island, Mobile County, with 200 slaves including Bambara – the first slaves to French Louisiana, on June 6, 1719, from Juda.

Another French ship, *Duc du Maine*, also arrived in 1719 at Dauphin Island (in present-day Mobile County, Alabama), this time with 250 slaves for French Louisiana. It too, came from Juda.

Between 1719 to 1728, six French ships left the slave port Juda to Louisiana:

Aurore	1719	200 slaves
Le Duc du Maine	1719	250 slaves
Afriquain	1721	182 slaves
Le Duc du Maine,	March 1721	349 slaves
Le Fortune	1721	303 slaves
La Diane	1728	464 slaves

After 1726, the Bambara arrived in Louisiana in large numbers. They were dispersed throughout Louisiana territory: New Orleans, Pointe Coupee Parish, Bienville Parish, Mobile (Alabama), Nathez (Mississippi), Illinois Country (Missouri, Illinois, Indiana), and to other plantation points in the territory.

The Louisiana Territory at that time stretched from parts of Canada and present-day Montana, Wyoming, Colorado, New Mexico, North & South Dakota, Minnesota, Iowa, Nebraska, Missouri, Kansas, Oklahoma, Arkansas, and New Orleans Territory.

Some Bambara names in Louisiana records between 1729 to 1752:

Biron, Changereau, Sabany, Malama, Antoine, Vulcain, Malborough, Sans Pour, Pierrot, Joseph, Mameurou, Bayou, Thomas.

The Bambara learned to speak French. There were many Bambara runaways. The Native Indigenous were held as slaves too by the French. Often in French Louisiana, Africans and Native Indigenous would runaway together, and try to find concealment among the Indigenous tribes in the countryside. Enslaved native Indigenous were also sent to the Caribbean to work the French sugar cane plantations. Numerous Indigenous tribes dotted the Louisiana region, such as the Blackfeet, Lakota Sioux, the Ottawa Potawatomi, the Miami Illinois, the Fox Sauk Kickapoo, the Biloxi, the Choctaw & Chickasaw, the Creek, Natchez, Quapaw, and the Chitimacha, to name a few. French soldiers engaged in slave raids on the Indigenous tribes. French Canadian soldiers, for example, raided the entire Chitimacha village on Bayou Lafourche, and sold the women and children into slavery.

There were also slave conspiracies. One such uprising was planned for June 29th, 1731. Several Africans of different nations were involved, including help from the Native Indigenous tribes. The Bambara agreed to join together with the plot. However, the plan was revealed to the French and so did not occur. It was said that up to four hundred Bambara were involved in the conspiracy.

Many slave runaway & enslavement cases are recorded in Louisiana's Court records involving the Bambara. Here are five examples:

July 1729 – a Bambara named Biron was charged with "Rebellion against his Master", and a Bambara interpreter named Samba said that Biron was only trying to prevent his master from shooting him with a gun while attempting to shackle him, and was not intending to attack his master. Biron was sentenced, whipped, and then returned to his master. **(Biron was one of the first Bambara enslaved in Louisiana. He arrived on the ship *Aurore* in 1719 from Juda/Whydah)**

December 7, 1743 – Runaway slaves, Malborough, of Bambara Nation, about 30 years old, Another Bambara about 28 years old; Michel of Fon Nation, about 45 years old.

1748 – Joseph, 30 years old, Bambara. He had run away several times from a plantation in New Orleans. Joseph was arrested and accused of theft. His master was Claude Joseph Dubreuil de Villars, one of the first French settlers in Louisiana. Dubreuil owned many slaves, and also sold some at a slave auction in September 1743. The Louisiana Census of 1746 reported Dubreuil as the richest plantation owner with 500 slaves. He owned several plantations, a sawmill, and a blacksmith shop. The name of his home was "Tchopitoulas Plantation" in New Orleans (the name came from an Indigenous tribal village "cote des Chopitoulas" which in Choctaw is believed to mean "Those who live by the River"), where Dubreuil grew cotton, indigo, and sugar cane. Dubreuil possibly purchased **the Bambara Joseph, who arrived from West Africa on the slave ship *Le St. Ursin* in 1743.**

May 1748 – Also on Dubreuil's plantation was a black slave named Cezard, who at night-time, along with his companion, an Indian slave woman named Angelique, would lead escaped slaves through the woods to the Choctaw nation to gain freedom. Cezard knew the woods well. He would have the escaped slaves wait in the woods for three days until the Choctaw arrived. Cezard also had taken a pirogue from Dubreuil.

(After Dubreuil's death in 1757, his entire estate was sold, along with the enslaved who were still left on the plantation)

July 1791 – In Pointe Coupee, a slave uprising involving the Mina and Bambara was planned to take place on July 9th. The plan was to kill the store owner Claude Trenonay, and then confiscate the firearms and ammunition to be used in the attack. However, several days prior, some of the Bambara slaves told their master George Pere Olivo about the plot, in which he then informed the officials that the slaves had scheduled a meeting for July 6th at New Roads in False River to discuss the plan. On the night of July 9th, the store owner Trenonay was killed by his Ibo slave, but the uprising did not come together as planned because many of the slaves had not been told when the meeting would be held. Also, on the evening of July 9th there was bad weather. A female slave named Venus was questioned about her contact with her neighbor Jaco, one of the three leaders of the plot. Venus said in her testimony that the Bambara were involved in the planned uprising, and that she didn't know anything about the plot until a slave named Digue told her. When Digue was questioned, he said he knew nothing about the plot until Venus had told him. All of Olivo's twenty-eight slaves had come from the Bight of Benin (**On the 1870 Federal Census of Louisiana, there are 425 freed people of color listed by name who reported they were born in "Africa". Many of**

these persons may very well be descendants of the Ewe and Bambara, and others from Hebrew West Africa).

Just as the Ewe people today, there is hardly any trace left of Hebrew Judaism among the Bambara. Today they are primarily Muslim.

France ceded Louisiana to Spain in 1762, and then after thirty-eight years of Spanish rule the Spanish ceded Louisiana back to France in 1802. Then France ceded Louisiana to the United States in 1803.

In former Benin Kingdom (now Southern Nigeria) lay "Igbo Country." Among the Igbo (Ebo/Eboe) today are Hebrew Igbo Jews who say they belong to the tribe of Gad. The tribe of Gad is one of the Twelve Tribes of Israel. Gad is also known as part of the ten tribe "Northern Kingdom" who split away from the two-tribe "Southern Kingdom" of Judah and Benjamin. The ten-tribes would later be conquered by Assyria in 740 BCE, deported to Assyrian cities within its empire (these cities later came under Persian rule), and became known as the Lost Ten Tribes of Israel.

Question: If the claim the Igbo Hebrews in Nigeria make is true, that they are of the tribe of Gad, then how did this tribe arrive in Africa? Or how could any of the twelve tribes for that matter? Does any documentation exist? In the previous book, *The Line of Shem and the Seed of Judah*, dozens of documented evidence was presented that among Hebrew Jews belonging to the twelve tribes, millions had moved to Africa. This chapter presents additional historical evidence – found in both the Bible and in Jewish rabbinical writings.

Within the Midrash *Pesikta Rabbati*, Chapter 31, regarding the whereabouts of the Lost Ten Tribes of Israel, it says this:

> To three places were the ten tribes exiled. Some were exiled to the Sambatyon River. Another group was exiled to a distant land behind the Sambatyon River; this land was

twice as far from Israel as the first. The third group was "swallowed in Rivlathah"..."To them that are in darkness, show yourselves" to those exiled to a distant land behind the Sambatyon River."

Reference is made to "the Sambatyon River," a legendary river whose location is uncertain, as being one of the places that the ten tribes were exiled by the Assyrians. Nahmanides says he identifies the river to be the Gozan River in Iran, which seems to harmonize with 1 Chronicles 5:26, where Ezra says some of the Israelites would be exiled to cities in Iran. Another location of the exiled ten tribes was in a land said to be twice as far from the Sambatyon River. **A third group of exiled ones is then said to be "in darkness"** and were "swallowed in Rivlathah," also an unknown region. Some scholars say "Rivalathah" is the town of Riblah in Syria, on the Orontes River. Obviously, more information is needed to ascertain these unknown locations. Notice how the *Jerusalem Talmud Sanhedrin*, Chapter 10, provides us more details:

> "To three places was Israel exiled: one to beyond the Sambatyon River, one to Daphne of Antiochia, **and one to where the clouds came down and covered them.** And when they shall return, so too will Reuben, Gad, and half of Manasseh return with them. How do we know all this? **From the verse in Isaiah** which states, "Say to the prisoners go forth" – these are those exiled Beyond the Sambatyon River." **To them that are in darkness, show yourselves – these are those upon whom the cloud descended and covered."**

Here we are given more detail. This time the first group of exiles are beyond the Sambatyon River, and the second group is said to be at Daphne of Antiochia, which is referring to Antioch, Syria. However, notice what is said about the third group, the ones who were said to be in darkness; the *Jerusalem Talmud Sanhedrin* says these are the ones "to where the clouds came down and covered them." It also quotes from a text cited in the Book of Isaiah. It is from Isaiah, chapter 49:

> "And he [Yah] proceeded to say: It has been more than a trivial matter for you to become my servant to raise up the tribes of Jacob and to bring back even the safeguarded ones of Israel…**to say to the prisoners, Come out! To those who are in darkness, reveal yourselves!** By the ways, they will pasture, and on all beaten paths their pasturing will be… Look! **These will come even far away**, and look! These from the north and from the west, and these **from the land of Sinim**." **(Isaiah 49:6, 9, 12)**

Isaiah foretold that scattered ones of Israel would be re-gathered from the land of Sinim. The Greek Septuagint renders the land of Sinim as the "Land of the Persians." However, the Targums and the Latin Vulgate render the text as "Land to the South," meaning *South of Israel* in the land of Canaan. What land or lands would be South of Israel in the land of Canaan? The lands of Egypt. In fact, modern scholars are suggesting the land of Sinim is referring to Syene (modern-day Aswan), the *Southern portion of Egypt* that is located on the east bank of the Nile across the island of Elephantine, where a large colony of Hebrew Jews existed on the border with Nubia-Cush. Notice what else Isaiah says about this African region:

"Woe to the land shadowing with wings, which is beyond the rivers of Ethiopia." (Isaiah 18:1)

Several scholars have made a connection to the reference "the land shadowing with wings" with the wings of the Tsetse fly of Ethiopia, while others point to the locust clouds of Ethiopia. Flying locust swarms are so powerful that clouds of them have actually blocked the light of the sun, as both Moses and the prophet Joel wrote:

"And the locusts went up over all the land of Egypt...for they covered the face of the whole earth, **so that the land was darkened**...They shall run to and fro in the city; they shall run upon the wall, they shall climb up upon the houses... **the sun and the moon shall be dark, and the stars shall withdraw their shining.**" (Exodus 10:14,15; Joel 2:9,10)

Could this be what was meant in the Jerusalem Talmud, that the exiles would "**be in darkness, where the clouds came down and covered them**"?

Other questions raised: Could the "land of Sinim" as mentioned in Isaiah 49 be referring to the "Kingdom of Semen" on Sanuto's map of 1588? Was the "Kingdom of Semen/Land of the Jews" an offshoot from the colony of Jews that once existed at Syene/Elephantine, Egypt during prophet Jeremiah's lifetime? There is a very strong possibility. The distance on foot from Aswan to Gondar would have been roughly three weeks time. Not far when considering almost the same distance the exiled Israelites took from Jerusalem to Elephantine.

One further document among the Jewish rabbinical writings, which shed light on whether the Tribe of Gad among the Igbo Hebrews of West Africa, or any other tribes of Israel came to live in

Africa, is the *Netzach Yisrael*, chapter 34, written by Sage Yehuda Loewe (Maharal of Prague) in 1599:

> "In the Talmud in chapter Chelek (Sanhedrin 94a) he said: To where were [the ten tribes] exiled? **Mar Zutra says: to Afrikei.** Now, according to the one who said "Afrikei," there are no known Israelites in Africa…the ten tribes are destined to return, the meaning is that they will return in the future along with the rest of the exiles, for even now also they are in the midst of the rest of the exiles, for originally He exiled them such that ultimately they would be able to return with the rest of the exiles, **for He exiled them originally to Afrikei or to the Selug Mountains.**"

Although he was of the opinion that there were no "known" Israelites in Africa in 1599, Sage Yehuda Loewe concedes that the Most High possibly did exile them originally to Africa. His peer, Mar Zutra, says the Israelites *were in Africa*. Additionally, this chapter has already laid out proof of this in the discussion about the "Land of the Jews" on the borders of Congo and Abyssinia, before, during, and after 1599. The writer Ogilby reported that the Land of the Jews/Kingdom of Semen was still there in 1670.

(Keep in mind too, that not all Israelites from the ten tribes followed Jeroboam into Idolatry, as several Hebrews from the ten tribes stayed loyal and joined Judah).

Between 1400 to 1865, an estimated 1.27 million slaves came from Igbo Country, and were imprisoned at the slave port Calabar in the Bight of Biafra. The first documented slave ship to reach Colonial Virginia from the port of Calabar, Benin Kingdom (Igbo) was on June 30, 1719. In fact, there were six ships that left Calabar and arrived in York, Virginia in the year 1719:

Date	Ship	Negroes	From whence imported
June 30th	Anne and Sarah	159	Calabar
July 9th	Little John	53	Calabar
July 25th	Berkley	183	Calabar
Aug. 18th	Sierralone	103	Calabar
Sept. 1st	Greyhound	170	Calabar
Sept. 8th	Colston	123	Calabar

The slave ship *Greyhound* made five trips from Calabar, Benin Kingdom (Igbo) to Virginia between 1719 – 1727, bringing 937 enslaved.

A ship named *Commerce* made four trips from Calabar, Benin Kingdom (Igbo) to Virginia between 1719 – 1726, bringing 906 enslaved. This same ship *Commerce* also made a trip in 1727 to Virginia, but only reporting it had left "Africa," and bringing 232 enslaved persons.

Between 1719 – 1769, a total of 39 slave ships came to Colonial Virginia from the slave port Calabar, Benin Kingdom (present-day Nigeria).

Olaudah Equiano **was kidnapped in 1756 from his Igbo village** of Essaka (in present-day Nigeria) and enslaved in Virginia, England, and the Leeward Islands. In his autobiography, Equiano stated that his Igbo tribe practiced the same customs of the Jews in the Torah. He was able to gain his freedom later in the United States.

John Brown was born a slave in Virginia sometime between 1810-1818 and later sent to Georgia. His grandfather was of the Igbo tribe. Brown states in his biography: "When in Slavery I was called Fed. I was raised on Betty Moore's estate, in Southampton County, Virginia. My mother belonged to Betty Moore. Her name was Nancy; but she was called Nanny. My father's name was Joe. He was owned by a planter named Benford, who lived in Northampton, in the same State. His father had been stolen from Africa. **He was of the Eboe tribe.**" (Sources, Chapter 15)

A slave named London in Savannah, Georgia, *translated the Book of John into Gullah using Arabic letters.* His birthplace is unknown. He died in Florida, where his slave owner later moved, sometime before 1858. During London's lifetime, it was speculated he was Mandingo. While the word *Mandingos* meant a people from a particular region in West Africa, the word was also a synonym for *African Muslims* in the minds of Southern whites.

This brings us to an aspect about Arabic-speaking slaves that is completely overlooked in this discussion: *Many Hebrew Jews had converted to Islam, and/or identified as Muslim before they arrived in America.* There are many accounts of nomadic Jews in Africa who were fleeing persecution from Muslims and fending off pressure to convert to Islam, or trying to maintain their Hebrew identity from assimilation into pagan-fetish tribes. Some were successful in retaining their Judaic heritage. But others were not. Over time, many Jews lost their Hebrew identity, and their descendants still observing pieces of their former customs and laws, but not understanding why. *They arrived in America as enslaved, but no longer identifying as Hebrew Jews. They came speaking Arabic and identified as Muslim.* Any semblance of a memory some still had remaining of their Hebrew Israelite identity, would in time fade away over generations, as loss of culture & more trauma sank in. Soon, even retaining Arabic would prove a challenge, let alone Hebrew or an Ethiopian language, unless in remote slave communities like the Gullah.

This is a strong solid reason why there are so few accounts found in America of enslaved Hebrew Jews *who identified as such.*

Here is another account – of a man enslaved in North Carolina:

Omar ibn Said was born about 1770 in his birthplace of Futa Toro, a Fulani district in Senegal. He identified himself as Fula and Muslim. As his autobiographical narrative in Arabic states, Omar was raised as a Mohammedan, learned Arabic, and in time taught Arabic and the prayers as a young man in his country. Omar became a dealer in cotton cloths. But one day around 1807, "there came to our place a large army who killed many men, and took me, and brought me to the great sea, and sold me," whereupon he was bound and put on a slave ship that landed in Charleston, South Carolina. Omar was sold to a slave owner, but escaped, ran away, and eventually was caught. While in jail, Omar began writing Arabic on the walls of the jail from coals he found in some ashes. He was sold to a slave holder named General Owens of Bladen County, North Carolina and spent the rest of his life there. The account includes a statement that the Owens family later in life gave Omar a copy of the Koran and the Bible, both in Arabic.

Omar ibn Said stated his birthplace was among the Fulani, or Fulas. Had the Fulas originally been Jews before they became Muslim? The book, *The Lost Tribes A Myth*, *by* Allen Godbey (1930), states that the Fulani have a tradition that they are descendants of Phut, one of the sons of Ham. Edmond D. Morel, in his book *Affairs of West Africa*, (published 1902), stated that the Fulani had a peculiar "knowledge of Jewish history." Quoting the French linguist De Guiraudon, the book goes on to state that the Fulani could not "have acquired their knowledge merely through Arabic sources... Moses and Abraham might have been individuals of the same race as themselves...it would seem as if the Puls (Fulani), if they themselves did not profess the Jewish faith...were at least in permanent contact with the Jewish people in remote times, and that, influenced at one time or another by the Israelites, they received Old Testament legends directly from them." We conclude with one last striking point by De Guiraudon about the Fulani: What they knew about Yeshua in the New Testament was very distorted, as if the message had reached them in a vague, fragmented condition.

Omar ibn Said acknowledged in his account, "General Jim Owen and his wife used to read the gospel...they read it to me very much...For the law was given by Moses but grace and truth were by the Jesus *the Messiah*."

Question: Had Omar heard about Yeshua when he lived in West Africa – or had he learned this for the first time, that Yeshua was the Messiah?

Another preserved account is that of Bilali Mohammed, an enslaved man on a plantation in Sapelo Island, Georgia during the American War of 1812. Bilali was Muslim, and could speak and write Arabic, but his first language was Fula.

In another account, Salih Bilali – born around 1790 near the Niger River in Massina, Mali – his enslaver estimated that around a dozen people spoke Fula on his plantation at St. Simons Island, Georgia during 1812. It is very possible that these enslaved Fulani who were brought to America were formerly Hebrews, or possibly their ancestors were.

It is documented the persecution Hebrews faced from Muslim tribes in Africa. For example, in 1492, when Askia Muhammed came to power in the region of Timbuktu, he decreed that Jews must convert to Islam or face expulsion. In 1526, the historian Leo Africanus wrote: "The king is a declared enemy of the Jews. He will not allow any to live in the city if he hears it said that a Berber merchant frequents them or does business with them he confiscates his goods." A nomad Jewish tribe called Daggatun, living in the Algerian Sahara as late as the 1850's, whose origins dated back to the 17ᵗʰ Century, had been pressured by the rulers of that region to convert to Islam, which they resisted. As a result, the Daggatun were exiled to the desert. Gradually they lost their Hebraic practices and eventually became Muslim. One ethnologist in the 1920's said that he "was unable to distinguish a Jew from a Mohammedan while passing along the streets of Algiers, Constantine, and Tunis. It is remarkable that among the non-Jewish natives there are seen many Jews of Negroid type." Without a doubt then, many of the enslaved who were brought to the American South were very likely Hebrews who had now begun to identify as Muslim.

There is something else further about the two enslaved men, London and Omar ibn Said. It is incredible how London was able to write English using Arabic characters to the Gullah dialect. William B. Hodgson, a world-leading philologist, and the person who received London's manuscript after his death, said this: "The manuscript of London is remarkable for precision in the use of the vowel points-harchat of the Arabic grammar...I infer from this, that as London was accustomed in making copies of the Koran with the same reverential sentiment he used the vowel points in copying the Bible of his adopted religion." Without doubt, both London and Omar ibn Said came from highly educated backgrounds. Both men could read and write Arabic. Did they both speak the same form of Arabic? Although the answer to that question is unknown, apparently there existed different forms of Arabic and dialects in the Middle Ages, and even in earlier times.

There was an eventual shift from predominant Hebrew-speaking to Arabic-speaking among Jews, as a result of the Muslim Conquest. Two forms of language that Jews spoke in early times, besides Hebrew, were *Judaeo-Spanish, and Judeo-Arabic*. Andalusi Romance was the main language spoken in Iberia before the Moors came in 711. However, gradually it was replaced by Andalusi Arabic during the rule of the Berber-Moors and Arab-Muslims. **By around 800 CE, most Jews within the Muslim Empire spoke Arabic.** *Judaeo-Spanish* was spoken in Moorish Spain before and after the Alhambra Decree of Expulsion. It incorporated many Hebrew, Aramaic, and Arabic words, and was spoken also in North Africa and in the Levant. *Judeo-Arabic dialects* were spoken by Jewish communities in the Arab world, and came about due to Hebrew words, and migration. (See Sources, Chapter 15)

So again, why were so few accounts *found* of enslaved Hebrews in America? Because by the time millions of enslaved Jews had arrived, **many of them were speaking Arabic, not Hebrew, and they no longer** *identified* **as being Hebrew Jews.** Why? *Because many no longer knew they were Hebrew, even though they were.* **Many had already begun identifying as Muslim** due to assimilation. (This also applies to Palestinians in the Gaza region today, as some of them had ancestors who were Hebrew Jews even though the majority of Palestinians identify as Arab Muslim).

Although direct evidence that London the slave was Hebrew is lacking, his story provides another very important insight into answering the question whether Hebrew Jews were part of the Trans-Atlantic Slave Trade passage to America.

London's story directs one to the language and culture of the Gullah people of the Georgia and South Carolina seaboard. How did the Gullah language originate? The people themselves, who have proudly carried and preserved the history and traditions of their culture for hundreds of years, have stated how the slaves, out of the various African regions from which they came, had to develop a form of communication amongst themselves. Thus, an amalgamation of words and phrases from the respective languages that each enslaved person possessed became, over time, one language, a collective language, their language. Researchers among the Gullah have traced the origin of some of their language words to Sierra Leone. Other researchers point to Angola as another original source.

Where Did the Word *Gullah* Itself Come From?

The word *Gullah* is found in the Hebrew language. In Hebrew, the word means "REDEEM." (LEVITICUS 25:24, 29, 32, 49)

Interestingly, the spiritual "Kum ba yah" is an African American spiritual known to be sung in the Gullah culture, with ties to enslaved West Africans.

The song was originally an appeal to God to come and help those in need.

There are many who say the phrase means: "COME BY HERE," meaning "PLEASE GOD COME HERE," a cry for help among those enslaved.

According to the book *Sweetgrass Baskets And The Gullah Tradition* by Joyce V. Coakley, the phrase "Bring Em Yuh" is translated "Bring It Here."

Another phrase, "Come Yuh or Been Yuh? can be translated, Have You Come To Visit Here, or You Been Here? In other words - Are You a Tourist or Resident?

The phrase "Kum Ba Yah" may also have another meaning. In the Gullah language, the title *Buh* or *Bah* is often added in front of a man's name to denote honor and kinship. So the spiritual "Kum Ba Yah" might actually be translated, "Come Great And Honorable Yah," since the word *Yah* in Hebrew is a shortened word for the Most High's personal name in scripture, Yahuah/Yahweh, (and Yahovah). Therefore, some Hebrew words found their way into the Gullah language. The word *Gullah* is Hebrew. And, Hebrew was a language spoken in Africa. Of course, we can expect there to be slight variations in accent and spelling. (See the book, *The Line of Shem and the Seed of Judah*)

Is there anything else in the Gullah culture which one can point to as additional evidence that Hebrews crossed Middle Passage? Absolutely. In the Hebrew Bible, the law to Israel in the Book of Leviticus, Chapter 25, verses 25-31, states that if an Israelite was to become poor and must sell his home and property, he or one of his family members should be given the chance to *"Gullah,"* or *"Redeem"* the land back. And that is exactly what the Gullah people do today. In South Carolina, when someone in the Gullah community loses their property to the City or State/County due to economic burden in paying delinquent property taxes, the auctioneer puts the real estate property up for public sale. During the bidding, a Gullah family member present at the auction will shout out, "Heir's property!" Upon hearing these words, the auctioneer pauses the bidding and explains to all potential buyers in attendance that the said real estate property in question belonged to descendants of enslaved people, and heirs will be allowed to claim their land. This old custom is called "Heirs rights" or "Redeeming the land." The Gullah people are repeating an ancient custom among the Hebrew Israelites. (Ruth 4:3,7) Coincidence?

We must be constantly reminded that one can never ignore or exclude the true history contained in the word of the Most High Yahuah, the Great Historian, and his accurate chronology. His holy calendar of prophetic events include the "Times of the Gentiles." The descendants of enslaved ancestors are looking for the answers as to where they are in the stream of time. They are searching as to *who they are.*

Will these descendants of their great-grandparents one day experience an awakening? Zephaniah 3:10 prophesied:

> *"From the region of the rivers of Ethiopia the one entreating me,*
> *the daughter of my scattered ones will bring a gift to me."*

What if those scattered from the region of the rivers of Ethiopia are scattered *further beyond* – as a result of being transported by means of slave ships? Would not they still be considered as the scattered ones? Absolutely. Everyone must be located and found, no matter where they are scattered.

Will the Most High allow time for them to learn about the Seed of Judah during the Messiah's Second coming? When would the Second Coming be?

Woman-Slave, Enslaved girl – New Orleans 1850

Bambara Girl

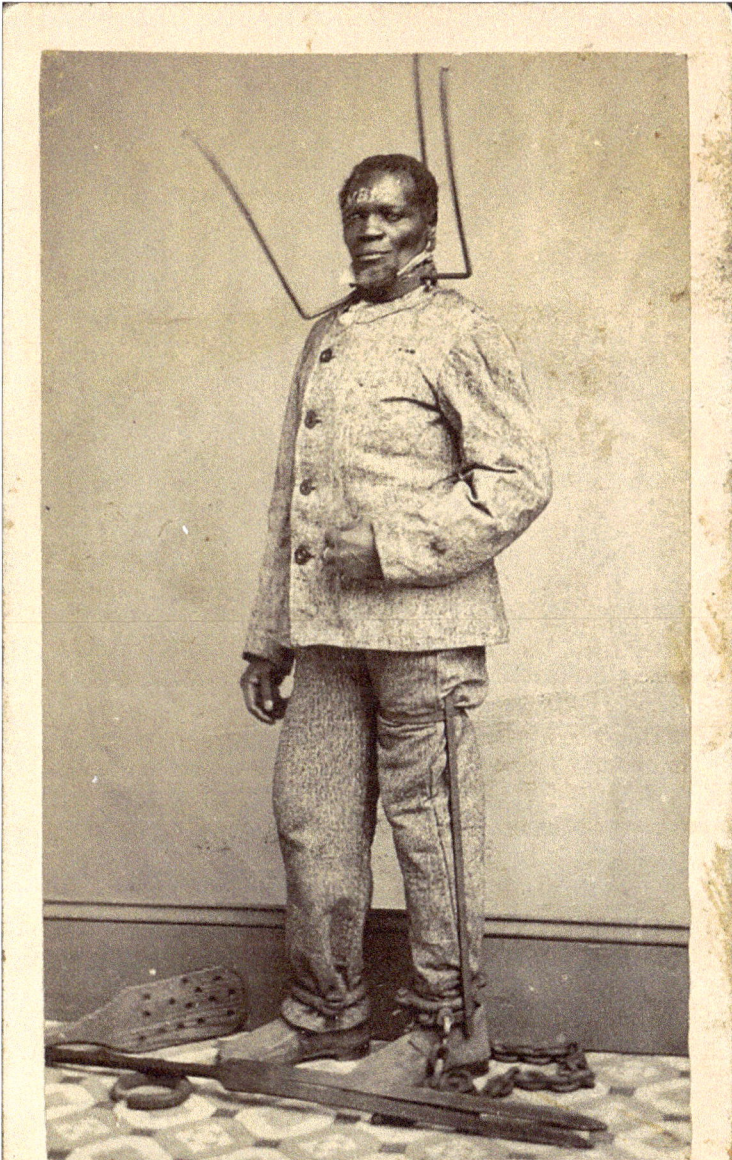

WILSON CHINN, a Branded Slave from Louisiana.

Photographed by KIMBALL, 477 Broadway, N. Y.

Entered according to Act of Congress, in the year 1863, by GEO. H. HANKS, in the Clerk's Office of the United States for the Southern District of New York.

Wilson Chinn a Branded Slave from Louisiana

Battlefield of Gettysburg

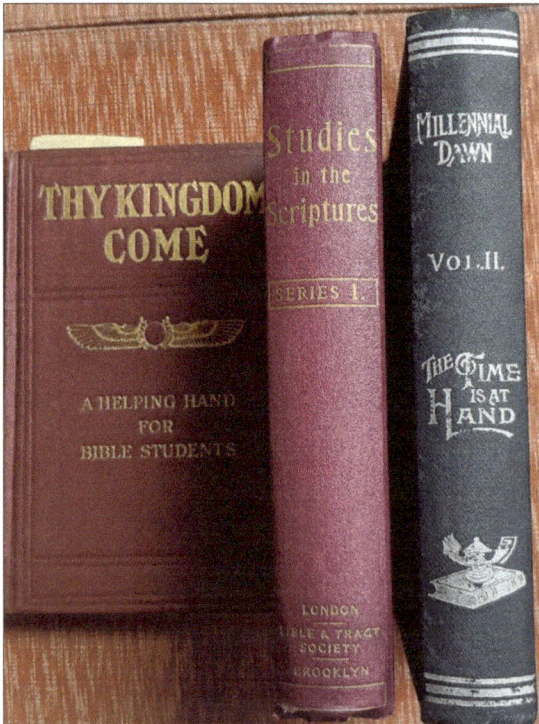

International Bible Students Discerned in the 1870's the Gentile Times would End in 1914

The Flight of the Prisoners. Babylon taking Judah, 607 BCE,
The Gentile Times Begin

Sweet Potato Planting, Hopkinson's Plantation 1862

Daily

Daily Net SALE Six Times as Large as That of Any Penny Lon

WEDNESDAY, AUGUST 5, 1914   **LONDON**   **MANCHESTER**

GREAT BRITAIN DECLARES WAR ON GERMANY

The following announcement was issued at the Foreign Office at 12.15 a.m.

'OWING to the summary rejection by the German Government of the request made by His Majesty's Government for assurances that the neutrality of

SUMMARY REJECTION OF BRITISH ULTIMATUM

Britain had sent an ultimatum to Germany which expired at midnight.

This was due to Germany's refusal to leave Belgium neutral and her invasion of that country.

The German Ambassador went to 10 Downing Street at 12.10am to receive his travel papers. He looked a broken man.

Sir Edward Goschen, the British Ambassador in Berlin, demanded his

Historic

Britain Declares War, 1914, The Gentile Times End

Negro Slaves 1862, Edisto Island, SC

Black Cotton-Farming Family (1890's)

Emancipated Slaves Brought from Louisiana

CHAPTER 16

The Times of the Gentiles and the King of Judah

As was said at the very outset of this journey, there is also a second ancient prophecy about a Coming Messiah – a Seed of Judah – who would make a second appearance. According to this prophecy the Messiah would arrive to be crowned "King" and would begin his "Kingdom." When would this happen? At the end of "the Gentile Times." Let us explore this fascinating forecast and see if any of it actually came true.

Just as in Chapter 10 we examined the centuries-old vision that predicted the Messiah's "first Coming" which would occur in the year 29, and which lined up amazingly accurate with verified historical events that calendar year, let us now get familiar with a second ancient revelation from the wise man Daniel in his Hebrew book, *which is said to give the "year" for the Messiah's second presence* (Dan 4:4,5,10-17,24,25,36). The scene is set – Daniel is called in by the king of Babylon to interpret a dream that the king had:

> "I, Nebuchadnezzar…there was a dream that I beheld, and it began to make me afraid…In the visions of my head while on my bed, **I saw a tree in the midst of the earth, and its height was enormous.** The tree grew and became strong, and its top reached the heavens, and it was visible to the ends of

the whole earth. Its foliage was beautiful, and its fruit was abundant, and there was food on it for all. Beneath it the beasts of the field would seek shade, and on its branches, the birds of the heavens would dwell, and all creatures would feed from it. As I viewed the visions of my head while on my bed, I saw a watcher, a holy one, coming down from the heavens. He called out loudly: "**Chop down the tree**, cut off its branches, shake off its leaves, and scatter its fruit! Let the beasts flee from beneath it, and the birds from its branches. **But leave the stump with its roots in the ground**, with a banding of iron and of copper, among the grass of the field. Let it be wet with the dew of the heavens, and let its portion be with the beasts among the vegetation of the earth. Let its heart be changed from that of a human, and let it be given the heart of a beast, *and let seven times pass over it*."

"This is by the decree or watchers, and the request is by the word of the holy ones, **so that people living may know that the Most High is Ruler in the kingdom of mankind _and that he gives it to whomever he wants_**, and he sets up over it even the lowliest of men."

"O king…you they will be driving away from men, and with the beasts of the field your dwelling will come to be…and seven times themselves will pass over you until you know that **the Most High is Ruler in the kingdom of mankind, _and that to the one whom he wants to he gives it_**."

As we just read, Nebuchadnezzar the king of ancient Babylon (who earlier had taken captive the Kingdom of Judah as slaves), had an intense dream about an enormous tree, which all of a sudden was chopped down, yet the stump of the tree was to be preserved for a period of "seven times." History books tell us that this king, Nebuchadnezzar, lost his sanity for seven literal years, but afterward regained his sanity and his reign was restored to the Babylonian throne. But does history tell us anything else? We must remember that this historical manuscript called the "Book of Daniel" which was written by the wise man himself, was not all about a king named Nebuchadnezzar who lost his sanity and acted like a literal wild beast. Shocking yes, but that was only a minor part of the story.

The main point is this: Babylon had taken the Most High's people captive as slaves. More importantly, Nebuchadnezzar had removed the Hebrew Israelite kings from off the throne of Judah! So this dream was not only about when Nebuchadnezzar would regain his rulership. That was only a minor fulfillment of the prophecy. *The real meaning of the dream has to do with when the Kingship of Judah would be restored.*

In the major meaning of this dream, the symbolic tree stands for the Israelite kings who represented the Most High God and His sovereignty here on earth. So when was that enormous tree in the dream chopped down?

It was in the year 607 BCE, when Nebuchadnezzar's Babylonian armies destroyed Jerusalem, interrupting the line of Israelite kings. When would the Israelite kingship be restored? Would that also be in 7 years just like it was for Nebuchadnezzar? No, the Israelite kingship was not restored in seven years after 607 BCE. In fact, there was never another *King*, an ancestral heir since 607 BCE who had received the ceremonial anointing as king to sit on the throne and restore the Judean kingship on earth. Why was that? The wise man Daniel said that the tree stump would be preserved for a specific time period – 7 times. This time period became known as the *Gentile Times*, when

"Jerusalem would be trampled by the nations" [Gentiles]. Then after this time period concludes, a royal heir would ascend to the throne to represent the sovereignty of God Yahuah/Yahweh. That was the meaning of the dream which wise man Daniel wrote down in Morse code. So this fact reveals that the "7 times" had a greater meaning than 7 literal years. These are 7 *prophetic years*.

So how long would the 7 prophetic years be? The scriptural pattern, or rule, is "a day for a year, a day for a year" (Numbers 14:34; Ezekiel 7:3). Unlike the prophecy of the "Seventy weeks," this prophetic dream has no mention of weeks, only of years. So by calculating the length of the7 times using the prophetic code of "a day for a year," we are presented with the mathematical equation of 360 times 7, since the Hebrew Jews counted in months of thirty days each (We can establish this by noting in the Book of Genesis that time was divided into months of thirty days (Genesis 7:11,24; Genesis 8:3,4; Revelation 12:6,14). At Deuteronomy 34:8, it says when Moses died the sons of Israel wept for thirty days. Even the Egyptians developed a calendar of lunar months of thirty days each). So, by calculating 360 days in a biblical year, multiplied by 7, we come to "2,520" days, and then by converting the days into years, we arrive at 2,520 *years* as the accurate length of the prophetic *seven times* in Nebuchadnezzar's dream. This was the Morse code that wise man Daniel wrote down.

The Israelite kingship was interrupted when Nebuchadnezzar captured King Zedekiah, the last Israelite king. Then Nebuchadnezzar replaced him with a man named Gedaliah, whom was appointed to be governor of the Hebrew land [but not king]. However, in the seventh month of Tishri of the Hebrew calendar [September-October] in 607 BCE, Gedaliah was assassinated, and the remaining patriots scattered, fleeing to Tahpanhes, Egypt for refuge, taking the prophet Jeremiah with them. **The land of Israel was now empty, bar-**

ren. (2 Kings 25:6, 7, 22, 25; Jeremiah 43:7,8). **The 2,520 years of the "Gentile Times" would begin counting then:** *Tishri, 607 BCE.*. Even Yeshua recognized, while he was living on earth in the 1st Century, that the Gentile Times would extend way into the future beyond his day when he said:

> "However, when you see Jerusalem surrounded by encamped armies, then know that the desolating of her has drawn hear…and they will fall by the edge of the sword and be led captive into all the nations, *and Jerusalem will be trampled on by the nations until the appointed times of the Gentiles are fulfilled." (Luke 21:24)*

It is beyond doubt that in *Tishri, 607 BCE* was when the 7 prophetic years began counting. Several historical sources establish that 537 BCE was when the Hebrew Jews returned to Judah, in fulfillment of another prophecy that the Jews would be in captivity for seventy years, as stated in the Book of Ezra. The *Encyclopedia Americana* states that the Book of Ezra covers the history of the returning exiles *"from 537 BC."* If one counts back 70 years from 537 BCE, they will arrive at 607 BCE, the year the "tree" was chopped down, when the Jews were taken from Judah and brought to Babylon. However, even after 537 BCE, when the Jews returned home to Judah, the throne of Judah still had not been restored. An Israelite named Zerubbabel was appointed as a *governor* of Judah (Haggai 1:1; 2:21), but no one has been appointed and made *king* of Judah in the physical city of Jerusalem to this day.

So just as Daniel had forecasted that the "Seventy Weeks" foretold when the Messiah would *first appear*, this revelation about the *seven times* is foretelling *when the Messiah would return, his second Coming*. Since the *seven times* is understood to mean a time period of 2,520 years (the Times of the Gentiles), we can logically discern that the Gentile Times would extend into the time period called "the Last Days" of the world. There is a connection between the Gentile Times and the Last Days. This is shown to be the case by looking at what else Yeshua said to his disciples that same hour he spoke to them about the Gentile Times. Yeshua was asked by his disciples, "Master, but when shall these things be? and what sign will there be when these things shall come to pass?" The disciples' question had been prompted because of what Yeshua had stated to them moments earlier. Yeshua revealed to them that the temple would be destroyed and disciples would be put to death:

> "And as some spake of the temple, how it was adorned with goodly stones and gifts, he said, As for these things which ye behold, the days will come, in the which there shall not be left one stone upon another, that shall not be thrown down... Nation shall rise against nation, and kingdom against kingdom, and great earthquakes shall be in divers places, and famines, and pestilences...But before all these, they shall lay their hands on you, and persecute you, delivering you up to the synagogues, and into prisons, and ye shall be betrayed both by parents, and brethren, and kinsfolks, and friends; and some of you shall they cause to be put to death." (Luke 21:5,6,10-12,16)

Some of the followers of Yahshua/Yeshua would be put to death. However, although persecution and Martyrdom would come about at the hands of political kings, soldiers, courts, even by friends and family members – who would be the *instigators* of those attacks on the original Hebrew and Greek-speaking Christians, those who were known as *The Way*? One of them would be the "Man of Lawlessness."

The Apostles Paul and Peter both wrote about this coming Apostasy, and Yahshua warned about it in his parable of the Wheat and Weeds.

This "Man of Lawlessness" is not an individual, but is a collective group, a revolt, a planned deliberate rebellion and apostasy. They are part of the serpent's seed. The Benjamite Paul foretold, "Let no one seduce you in any manner, because it will not come unless the apostasy comes first and the man of lawlessness gets revealed, the son of destruction, and lifts himself up over everyone who is called god or an object of reverence, so that he sits down in the temple of The God, publicly showing himself to be a god…but the lawless one's presence is according to the operation of Satan with every powerful work and lying signs and portents…" (2 Thessalonians 2:3,4,9)

The Apostle Peter also alerted the disciples, "There will also be false teachers among you. These very ones will quietly bring in destructive sects and will disown even the owner that bought them, bringing speedy destruction upon themselves."(2 Peter 2:1) Yeshua warned his followers of this coming apostasy in his parable about "the Wheat and the Weeds" when he said:

> The kingdom of the heavens has become like a man that sowed fine seed in his field. While men were sleeping, his enemy came and over sowed weeds in among the wheat… the slaves of the householder came up and said to him, Master, did you not sow fine seed in your field? How, then, does it come to have weeds? He said to them, an enemy, a man did this. They said to him, Do you want us, then, to go out and collect them? He said, No…**let both grow together until the harvest**, and in the harvest season I will tell the reapers, First collect the weeds and bind them in bundles

to burn them up, then go to gathering the wheat into my storehouse." (Matthew 13:25-30)

The other instigator who would incite persecutions and deaths upon the followers of Yeshua, and twist the truth of his teachings, is the one mentioned in Revelation as "Babylon the Great":

"the great prostitute…with whom the kings of the earth committed sexual immorality…a woman…upon a scarlet colored beast, full of names of blasphemy, having seven heads and ten horns. And the woman was arrayed in purple and scarlet colour, and decked with gold and precious stones and pearls, having a golden cup in her hand full of abominations and filthiness of her fornication, and upon her forehead was a name written, MYSTERY, BABYLON THE GREAT, THE MOTHER OF HARLOTS AND ABOMINATIONS OF THE EARTH." (Revelation 17: 3-5)

We notice in this vision that the Apostle John saw, that Babylon the Great is a symbolic woman, a harlot, prostituting her sexual tricks with "the Kings of the earth." The reason why this harlot is called "Babylon the Great" is because she promotes and teaches false religious worship, all the false religious pagan customs and teachings that began in ancient Babylon Chaldea, such as triune gods and goddesses, talking to dead ancestors, teachings of an immortal soul, eternal hellfire, the crucifix, a clergy priesthood, and many more myths and tales from the crypt (For example, the Most High says that the dead are not conscious of anything, they go back to the ground, their thinking is no more, and their soul dies. Yahshua says that death is likened to sleep. *Death* is the "opposite" of *Life*. Ecclesiastes 9:5, 10; Psalms 146:4; Ezekiel 18:4; John 11:11-14)

Also notice in the vision that this symbolic woman "Babylon the Great" is riding a scarlet-colored "wild beast." This beast symbolizes all the kings of the earth, the entire political system of the earth, who does the bidding of the prostitute. So many horrible things have been done in the name of so-called "Christianity," so much bloodshed, hatred, and hypocrisy. It is little wonder that millions have turned away from "Christianity" and religion in general.

But, as was mentioned in the preceding paragraphs, **all this warring and hatred in the name of religion can be blamed on "Christendom" – the foretold Apostasy** and "Man of Lawlessness", *not the true original Hebrew disciples of Yahshua/Yeshua who were known as The Way.* In fact, in the Bible book called "Acts of the Apostles" is recorded when the original Hebrew disciples of Messiah Yeshua started for the first time to "be called Christians." (Acts 11:26) The Greek word for "Called" is *Chrematizo.* According to W.E. Vine's *Expository Dictionary of New Testament Words*, pg 31, it says that the word *Chrematizo,* "came to signify the giving of a **Divine admonition** or instruction or warning in a general way…Names were given to men from the nature of their business." So in the Bible book Acts of the Apostles, the first time Yeshua's disciples were called Christians, **it implies divine direction or revelation by God.** Hence, several Bible translations render Acts 11:26 as "*by divine providence* were called Christians." So the original Hebrew and Greek followers of Yahshua/Yeshua in the 1st Century would be known by two scriptural names, The Way, and also as "Christians", which in Hebrew is *Meshichiyim*, Messianists. *Before* the Apostasy of Christendom began. So there is a distinction between "Christendom", a false apostatized form of religion, and "true Christians" who embrace the original teachings of Yeshua/Yahshua.

Turning our attention again to the mysterious woman, Babylon the Great – if the grotesque scene of a prostitute riding a seven-headed wild beast with ten horns was not shocking enough, then notice the next scene presented in this revelation regarding this unclean harlot:

> "And I saw that the woman *was drunk with the blood of the holy ones and with the blood of the witnesses of Yeshua.*" (Revelation 17:6)

This false religious worldwide system, Babylon the Great, has instigated and provoked gross amounts of religious and political hatred on the Hebrew and Greek-speaking followers of Yahshua/Yeshua. Note a few historical sources (See Sources, Chapter 16) that show how the original Hebrew Christians were treated during the Roman Empire while under the influence and control of the harlot:

A great fire erupted in Rome in 64 CE, destroying one fourth of the city. According to historian Tacitus, it was rumored that Emperor Nero was responsible, and to protect himself blamed the original Christians. This resulted in mass arrests of Yeshua's followers, who were tortured, many put to death, and some burned alive.

Christians refused sacrifice to the emperor, and very few of the Christians recanted. All a prisoner had to do was scatter a pinch of incense on the flame and he would be given a Certificate of Sacrifice and turned free. It was also carefully explained to him that he was not worshipping the emperor, merely acknowledging the divine character of the emperor as head of the Roman state. Still, almost no Christians availed themselves of the chance to escape.

The first Christians thought it was wrong to fight, and would not serve in the army even when the Empire needed soldiers.

Christians refused to enter the army or to take any part in war. Origen remarked that Christians could not engage in war against any nation. They have learned from their leader that they are children of peace. In that period many Christians were martyred for refusing military service.

The early Christians were arrested and flogged for preaching from house to house, as Yeshua had trained them to do.

The Benjamite Hebrew Paul was put to death during the rule of Nero, sometime between 65-68 CE

What was the penalty when courageous persons made the Bible available for the common folk on the street to have access to read it, or if anyone questioned the Papacy:

John Wycliff, a Bible translator, questioned the Papacy. Wycliff believed in translating the Bible into the common Vernacular so people could read and study it. After Wycliff's death in 1384, Pope Martin V confirmed that his corpse be exhumed and his bones to be burned. His ashes were done away with in the River Swift in 1428, forty-four years after Wycliff's death.

William Tyndale, a translator of the Bible into English, which infuriated the Papacy, whose policy was against the common people reading or possessing a Bible. Tyndale was arrested, and in 1536 was convicted of heresy, executed by strangulation, and then burnt at the stake.

Michael Servetus, a Spanish theologian and physician. He rejected the Trinity and other unscriptural doctrines and was condemned by the Papacy. Servetus was burned at the stake in 1553.

Just as Yeshua had said in answer to the question his disciples had asked about the sign of his second return or presence, persecution of his followers would continue in the last days. In his parable of the wheat and weeds, Yeshua said that both will grow together until the "harvest," which he said meant "is a conclusion of a system of things" (or End of the world; End of the age, Matthew 13:39).

So the Gentile Times has a direct connection and bearing on the time period referred to as the "End of the world." In fact, the Gentile Times has a direct connection to the Book of Revelation, since that book covers the events of the "Last Days" in symbolic language. What was the whole point of Nebuchadnezzar's dream? It was that after 7 times had passed, the royal kingship of Judah would be restored, and, as the dream indicated, *"so that people living may know he gives it (the Kingdom) to whomever he wants."* Notice the Most High's choice as to **who would restore the royal kingship?** When the seventh angel blew his trumpet, Revelation 11:15 says:

> "And the seventh angel blew his trumpet. And loud voices occurred in heaven, saying: The Kingdom of the world did become the Kingdom of our Lord and of his Christ (Messiah), and he will rule as king forever and ever."

This text is referring to the coronation of Hamashiach!

This Biblical vision in the Book of Revelation tells us that the royal kingship is finally restored at the end of the Gentile Times by Yeshua/Yahshua the Messiah IN HEAVEN.

How long is the Gentile Times, and when would it end? We have already established that Nebuchadnezzar's dream of "7 times" is a prophetic time period of 2,520 years, counting from 607 BCE when the Hebrew Jews of Judah were taken captive to Babylon, and the royal kingship of Judah was temporarily cutoff until the time period of 2,520 years ends. When would that be? From 607 BCE, 2,520 years would end in 1914 CE.

Is there evidence that the true Mashiach returned in the year 1914 and restored the royal kingship as foretold by the wise man Daniel the prophet? Yes, there is.

- In the vision of the 4 horsemen of the Apocalypse in Revelation chapter six, the rider of the white horse was given "**a crown.**" (Rev. 6:2)

- The 4 horsemen rider of the red horse "took peace away from the earth, so that they would slaughter one another; and a "great sword" was given him." (Rev. 6:4)

- Yeshua said that at the time of his second return, "Nation shall rise against Nation, and Kingdom against Kingdom." (Matt. 24:6)

- When the seventh angel blew his trumpet, loud voices in heaven announced, "**the Kingdom of the world did become the Kingdom of our Lord and of his Christ (Messiah), and he will rule forever and ever.**" (Rev. 11:15)

- After loud voices in heaven announced the Kingdom of the Lord's Messiah (Christ), **a war broke out in heaven** and the one called Devil and **Satan and his angels were thrown down to the earth.** (Rev. 12:7-12)

- **In Sept/Oct 1914 (the Hebrew month of Tishri), World War I began. At that time, historians called it the "Great War" because no war of that kind had ever occurred before in terms of its size and modern weaponry.**

- The final overthrow of Judah by Nebuchadnezzar occurred in the month of Tishri, 607 BCE, when the land of Judah became barren. **So the Times of the Gentiles (2,520 years) ended accurately right on time in 1914, to the very month!**

• The Messiah's Return was to be an invisible presence, based on Matthew 24:3, where it says the "Sign of your *Parousia*" in the Greek translations. The Greek word *Parousia* means "Presence", as having Come, Arrived; not "coming", as "on the way." (If someone is *physically* present, there is no need for a "Sign").

Conclusion: Yeshua/Yahshua is the true Messiah. He was a direct descendant of Judah, according to ancient Jerusalem's public genealogy records (Mathew, Chapter One; Luke, Chapter Three). Yeshua restored the royal kingship of Judah by sitting on the throne in Tishri, 1914, the exact ending of the Gentile Times to the very month, and ruling invisibly from his throne in Heaven to gather together all people who recognize the *truth* about him in these Last Days.

Another key major prophetic development that occurred in 1914 was what is mentioned in the Book of Revelation, Chapter 17, verses 9 & 10:

"Here is where the intelligence that has wisdom comes in; The seven heads mean seven mountains, where the woman sits on top. And there are seven kings: five have fallen, one is, *the other has not yet arrived, but when he does arrive he must remain a short while.*"

The disciple and Apostle John penned those words while being instructed to do so from an angel that Yeshua/Yahshua had sent to John. Speaking of seven kings or seven world empires, John wrote that five of them had already fallen, which were Egypt, Assyria,

Babylon, Medo-Persia, and Greece. Why only these empires? Were there not many other mighty world powers in history? Yes. However, the seven empires or "kings" that John was referring to were ones which involved the Most High's covenant people throughout time. John goes on to mention of the sixth king – "one is" – meaning the Roman Empire, which was ruling in John's lifetime.

But then John says, *"the other has not yet arrived, but when he does arrive he must remain a short while."* This is referring to the 7th king. Who is it? It is the world power that came shortly after 1914 when World War I began, namely *the Anglo-American World Power – Great Britain and the United States of America, a dual-world power.* To this day, the Anglo-American World Power (although not without very strong competition from Russia, China, and other coalition of nations, i.e. "king of the North." See Sources, Chapter 16) dominates the entire earth politically, militaristically, and financially. *They are a racial empire with the goal of maintaining global dominance.* Here is one example highlighting this fact. The next year, 1915, while the First World War was still raging, a shocking motion picture was released. **It was a silent film called "*The Birth Of A Nation*."** The film portrayed the Ku Klux Klan, a white supremacist hate group, as a "positive moral force" for "vigilante justice." The first public showing of the film was on January 1, 1915, and the film's original title at that time was called *The Clansman*. It was even shown in the White House on February 18, 1915 with President Woodrow Wilson, his family members, and his governing cabinet present. By January 1916, an estimated over 3 million people had watched the film. The film was based upon a novel, *The Clansman*, written in 1905 (See Sources, Chapter 16). So the film, The Birth of a Nation is just one example showing the mentality and psychology of the Anglo-American dual world power, the 7th head of the Wild Beast in Revelation, whose sole purpose is global sovereignty of Earth, in opposition to the Most High's appointed Mashiach king, Yeshua/Yahshua. Even now, efforts are being put forth by the 7th head of the beast to rewrite history. However, there is one thing they cannot do: They cannot erase how the prophetic word of the Most High is being fulfilled. Yet, mankind will shudder at what the wild beast is planning to soon do, as will be explained in the next chapter.

So, did anyone make public media announcement that the Gentile Times would end in 1914? Yes, a millennial Bible study group in the late 19th century called the "International Bible Students." *By 1876, the Bible Students understood that the Gentile Times mentioned in Daniel's prophecy was 2,520 years long and would end in 1914.* **In 1914, the International Bible Students produced a "talking movie" called "*The Photo-Drama of Creation,*" which was a combination of motion pictures and a slide presentation, synchronized with sound. This "talking" motion picture was ahead of its time, and seen by millions around the world, drawing attention to the year 1914** as the year they believed the Messiah Jesus would return for his chosen ones. By just the end of 1914, over 9 million had seen it in North America, Europe, and Australia. The Bible Students also published this understanding in their publications and distributed them worldwide in several languages. Some of their pamphlets would say, 'The times of the Gentiles would expire with the year 1914' and 'the Times of the Gentiles will run fully out with the year A.D. 1914, when Christ's Kingdom would be established' (publications between 1876 to 1914).

The International Bible Students felt it was important that they dedicate themselves to returning to the original teachings of Yeshua/Yahshua. They also were very committed to understanding Bible prophecy, especially in relation to the Lord's Second Coming.

This Bible group had rejected all of the mainstream "apostatized Christian" religions. They felt that these apostatized religions were promoting pagan babylonish beliefs in their church doctrines, such as hellfire, the Trinity, Immortality of the Soul, and other teachings that were not taught by Yeshua/Yahshua and his early followers in the 1st Century. The International Bible Students felt it was important that they root out any such pagan customs as soon as it was discerned from the Bible. In 1933, the International Bible Students became known as "the Witnesses of Jehovah/Yahowah," based on the Hebrew text at Isaiah 43:10: "Ye are my witnesses, saith Yahovah."

Right now as of this book release, the Witnesses of Jehovah are persecuted and being thrown into prison in the East African country of Eritrea. Why? Following the commandments of Yahshua and not supporting military war or taking political sides. They are only trying to live peaceful lives. Also in the country of Russia, hundreds of them are being arrested and sentenced to long prison terms. Why? Again, following the commandments of Yahshua by not supporting military war or taking political sides. They are only trying to live as peaceful citizens. The Witnesses of Jehovah/Yahowah are also banned or restricted in over thirty other countries, for the same reasons. During World War Two, Nazi Germany under Hitler arrested 6,262 witnesses of Jehovah/Yahowah, and 2,074 were sent to concentration camps.

Yahshua said, "You will be hated by all the nations on account of my name."

The days we are now living in are very challenging. Today there is War, Suffering, Oppression, Hatred. There is Racism, Sickness, Homelessness, Hunger. And there is Crime, Greed, and power-grabbing tyrants. Yeshua/Yahshua pointed to this as "the last days," or "Conclusion of the system of things."

So what are we to do?

CHAPTER 17

Who Are the Gentiles In Paul's Letters, and Who Are the Edomites?

The Greek word for the term Gentiles is Ethnos, referring to a multitude of people of the same nature or group, a nation, a people. In a general sense, a nation is made up of people who are related to one another by blood and/or have a common language, a defined geographic territory, a distinct culture, and adhere to some form of laws and governing body.

The term Gentiles in the biblical text refers to anyone who was non-Jew, a person or people who had not dedicated themselves to the worship and obedience to Yah. In the 1st century, during the time of the Roman Empire, the term Gentiles came to be applied by Jews to persons who were Greek, or who spoke the Greek language. Thus, the terms Greek and Gentile became interchangeable terms.

The Apostle Paul in his letters to the early congregations mentioned often about the Jews/Israel and the Gentiles. One of his letters about Israel and the Gentiles has been the center of much study and debate, and found in his letter to the Hebrew Christian congregation in Rome, called the "Letter to the Romans." In his discussion to the congregation, Paul makes mention of an illustration about two olive trees – a wild olive tree and a garden olive tree. Paul goes on to illustrate that some of the natural branches of the garden olive tree had been broken off, and so the broken branches would be grafted back into the tree. But, branches from the wild olive tree would also be grafted into the garden olive tree. Then Paul makes the point that the branches from both trees represent two groups of people (Romans 11:17-24).

So the questions now become: **Who are those who represent the branches from the wild olive tree which are grafted into the garden olive tree?** And who are those who represent the natural branches and are grafted back into its own tree?

Paul makes it clear that the natural branches which are grafted back into their own garden olive tree are the Hebrew Jews – because they originally received the promises from the Most High and were in a covenant relationship with Him. That part is true. So who represents the other group, the wild olive tree? **Are they the ten-tribe Northern kingdom who broke away from the two-tribe Southern kingdom of Judah and Benjamin? Is that what Paul is saying?**

Some who accept this view cite the prophecy in Ezekiel, Chapter 37, where Ezekiel is told by the Most High to take two sticks, and to write on one stick "for Judah" and on the other stick "for Joseph, the stick of Ephraim." Then Ezekiel is told to bring the two sticks together in his hand, "so that they become one stick." This prophecy was foretelling when the ten-tribe Northern kingdom which had broken away from the two-tribe kingdom of Judah and Benjamin would reunite again to become "one kingdom." However, in regards to what Paul wrote to the Hebrew congregation about the two olive trees, some people today hold the view that the "unfaithful ten-tribes" represent the branches of the wild olive tree that will be grafted in, and the "two-tribes" represent the natural garden olive tree, and that this fulfills the prophecy of Ezekiel regarding the two sticks. Is this view accurate? No, and here is the reason why.

The prophecy in Ezekiel about the two sticks was already fulfilled in 537 BCE. Because that was when the Twelve Tribes of Israel reunited, when they left the realm of Medo-Persia and Babylon, and returned to Jerusalem to restore the worship of Yah and begin the work of rebuilding the temple. In 539 BCE, Cyrus the Great and his armies overthrew the empire of Babylon. When that occurred, not only did Cyrus allow the Hebrews from the two-tribes who were slaves in Babylon to return to Jerusalem, but his defeat of Babylon also paved the way for the Hebrew descendants of the ten-tribes who were slaves in the former districts of Assyria to leave for Jerusalem too. This is shown by Cyrus' edict of 539 BCE, and the Cyrus Cylinder. Two years later in 537, exiled Jews arrived in Jerusalem. Some of those former districts and cities of Assyria were now under Persian control (some of the ten-tribes were sent to cities in Iran). Notice what 1 Chronicles and the Book of Ezra reports:

"And in Jerusalem there dwelt some of the sons of Judah and some of the sons of Benjamin *and some of the sons of Ephraim and of Manasseh settled in Jerusalem*…and they presented for the inauguration of this house of God a hundred bulls, two hundred rams, four hundred lambs, and as a sin offering *for all Israel twelve male goats, according to the number of the tribes of Israel."* (1 Chronicles 9:3; Ezra 6:17)

So both the stick of Judah and the stick of Ephraim came together as one stick, in fulfillment of Ezekiel's prophecy, when a remnant of all twelve tribes returned to Jerusalem in 537 BCE. **Ezekiel's prophecy does not mention that one stick is broken in half** and then brought together as one. It says there will be two sticks.

On the other hand, Paul mentions that branches **would be broken off**, and then grafted together. The tribes of Israel received the promises, but most of them tried to attain righteousness by works of the Law. When Messiah Yeshua/Yahshua appeared, they rejected him, leading to the Most High breaking them off as branches on a garden olive tree. Paul's letter to the congregation was trying to help them see a public declaration of faith in Yahshua is what leads to salvation, not works of the Law (Romans 9:27-33). Paul says:

> "A dulling of senses has come upon Israel **until the full number of people of the nations [Gentiles] has come in**, *and in this manner* all Israel will be saved." (Romans 11:25, 26)

Therefore in this text, "Israel" is referring to, not an Israel dependant upon tribal birth affiliation but, *a Spirit-begotten Israel*, made up of Hebrews (branches grafted back) AND people of the nations (branches from the wild olive tree) who both follow the Messiah Yahshua (Romans 2:28,29; Acts 10:15, 34).

What about the Samaritans? The Samaritans, because of their acceptance of the Pentateuch (the first five books of the Hebrew Scriptures), they have been given a basis for believing that the Messiah would come. In the 1st Century, Samaritans were looking for him. Yahshua revealed himself to the Samaritan woman at the water-well, and as a result many of the Samaritans put faith in Yahshua (John 4:25, 26, 39-42).

The Edomites:

Who is Edom? Edom was the second name for Esau, the twin brother of Jacob. Esau's parents were Isaac and Rebekah. **Esau's grandfather was Abraham.**

How did Esau get the name Edom? Because he sold his birthright to his brother Jacob over a bowl of red stew (Genesis 25:30-34). Another fact, although not having to do with his name, Esau at birth had a very red hue. This red hue also was passed down to his later descendants.

Did Esau/Edom and his offspring descend from Japtheth? No. **Esau/Edom was Semitic**, having descended from the line of Shem, through Abraham and his father Isaac. **Esau's descendants the Edomites were Semitic and part Hamitic**, because of his wives.

What were the Edomites primarily known for? They built up a gross reputation of being staunch enemies of the Israelites by the way they treated the people of Israel in biblical history.

What happened to the Edomites? About the middle of the Sixth Century BCE, the Babylonians under King Nabonidus conquered their lands Edom and Tema. By the Fourth Century BCE, the Edomites moved to Hebron and then later to the southern part of Judea which became known as Idumea. According to Josephus, Maccabean ruler John Hyncanus I gained control over them and compelled the Edomites to convert to Judaism around 120 BCE. Some of the Edomites were a family of political rulers known as Herod.

Where are the Edomites/Idumeans today? There is no active nation, current geographic place, or people who identify as such today. They were a Semitic and Hamitic people, not Caucasian. Some say they were absorbed into the area of the Middle East, perhaps in the Jordan region. They vanished from history after the destruction of Jerusalem in 70.

Are the Edomites blood related to the Macedonians or the Khazars? No. Some confuse the father and grandfather of Herod the Great, Antipater, with Antipater the Greek regent of Macedonia, but there is no connection. Likewise, there is no direct evidence or historical claim that the Edomites were related to the Khazers. The Edomites were a Semitic/Hamitic people who lived in the region of Edom and

Idumea. The Khazers, who formed an empire in the Caucasus region, were a Turkic/Japhetic people, as also were the Macedonians.

What does the name Edom symbolize in the Biblical context? The name Edom in prophetic scripture symbolize the enemies of the Most High and of His people. He has denounced forever all those who fit into the "Edom" category (Malachi 1: 1-4; Obadiah 10, 18).

Are Paul's letters trustworthy?

Yes absolutely. Some today try to cast doubt on Paul's writings, even saying it was the Roman Catholic Church who decided his letters to be included in the Bible. Even though the Roman Catholic Church "makes claims" that they were responsible as the sole arbiter to the Bible canon at the Council of Carthage in 397, it is far from the truth. There are a number of early catalogs of the Greek Scriptures (New Testament) that date hundreds of years prior to that council, and which show universal acceptance in the early congregations the same books as found in the New Testament today. Some examples being the early New Testament catalogs of Irenaeus, Clement, Tertullian, Origen, and Eusebius.

CHAPTER 18

What We Need To Do Now
Do I Have to Move to Africa to be Saved?

"Out of Egypt I Called My Son" (Matthew 2:15)

Is there an "Ingathering" taking place right now of dispersed people during the royal reign of Yeshua Hamashiach? Yes! Yeshua/Yahshua said:

> "And they will fall by the edge of the sword, **and will be led captive into all the nations**; and Jerusalem will be trampled on by the Nations **until the Times of the Gentiles are fulfilled.**" (Luke 21:24)

We recall the context of Yeshua's words were in relation to when the temple in Jerusalem would be surrounded and destroyed by Roman armies, and Hebrew Jews would be captured and sold as slaves. Notice Yeshua said that Hebrew Jews would be *led captive into all the nations*. The Greek word for nations is *Ethnos*, where we get the word *ethnic*. So Hebrew Jews would be led captive into *All the basic ethnic regions of the world*: Africa, Asia, Europe, the islands of the sea, *AND the Americas*. The Greek phrase *aichmalotos* in the Greek language of that New Testament scriptural text means "They will be led captive." Strong's Concordance says of aichmalotos, **"Prisoner of war; To make captive, lead away captive; bring into captivity."** So to be clear – we are not talking about voluntary immigration. We are talking about prisoners of war. The rest of Yeshua's words said, "into all the nations." The Greek word "into" in this context is *eis*, which means "the point reached or entered." The Greek word that Yeshua used for the word "all" is *panta*, and means "in all places everywhere."

Can you think of a time when "Hebrew Jews" were ***led captive as slaves into the Americas?***

We are living in exciting times right now. All over the world, people are studying the Bible more than ever and trying to understand the meanings of these ancient prophecies. Why is this happening especially now in this 21st Century? The Most High said through his prophet Isaiah that He would re-gather His dispersed ones back:

"And it must occur in that day that Yahuah will again offer his hand a second time, to acquire the remnant of his people who will remain over from Assyria and from Egypt and from Pathros and from Nubia-Cush, and from Elam and from Shinar and from Hamath and from the islands of the sea. And he will certainly raise up a signal for the nations and gather the dispersed ones of Israel, and the scattered ones of Judah he will collect together **from the four corners of the earth**." (Isaiah 11:11,12)

> We are living in a special time than no other. The Most High is giving the descendants of those ancestors who were once in a covenant relationship with Him one more opportunity to come back and become part of the new arrangement He has established when the Gentile Times ended. The Most High is a loving God. He does not want anyone to lose *life*.

> Yeshua, when on earth, carried out his assignment that his father the Most High had given him regarding the lost sheep. We recall when Yeshua/Yahshua entered the region

of Tyre and Sidon and encountered a woman who was not a Hebrew:

"And, look! A Canaanite woman from those regions came out and cried aloud, saying: "Have mercy on me, Lord, Son of David. My daughter is badly demonized…In answer he said: I was not sent forth to any but to the lost sheep of the house of Israel." (Matthew 15:22-24)

Yeshua's assignment while on earth was to minister to the lost sheep of the house of Israel. It was not yet time to minister and baptize people of the nations, the Gentiles. That assignment would come later. According to Daniel's prophecy of the Seventy Weeks, it would be at the end of the "one week" when the "covenant with Abraham" would widen out to include others, and a new assignment would begin – making disciples from people of all the nations, while becoming circumcised and observing the Law Covenant would no longer be a requirement to gain the Most High's approval (Daniel 9:27). Such was the case with the Italian Cornelius who was not a Hebrew Israelite or proselyte. (Acts of the Apostles, chapter 10)

Daniel 9:27 says:

"And he shall confirm the covenant with many for **one week**: and in the middle of the week he shall cause the sacrifice and gift offering to cease"

Yeshua/Yahshua was put to death in 33 CE, in the middle of the "one week," which began in 29 CE when Yeshua was baptized and became the Messiah. The end of the "one week" was 36 CE, and the completion of the "Seventy years" prophecy (See Chapter 12). The blessings of the covenant that the Most High made with Abraham would be extended to Abraham's Hebrew offspring "one week." **Then at the end of the "one week," Yehovah's covenant with Abraham would extend an invitation to the nations.** When the invisible Yahuah told Peter, "Stop calling defiled the things God has cleansed," Peter responded, *"God is not partial, but in every nation the man who fears him and does what is right is acceptable to him"* (Acts 10:15-48).

But that new arrangement had not yet started when Yahshua was on earth. However, the Canaanite-Phoenician woman was persistent. The account continues:

> "When the woman came she began doing obeisance to him, saying: Lord, help me! In answer he said: it is not right to take the bread of the children and throw it to *little dogs (kunarion)*." She said, Yes, Lord, but really the *little dogs (kunarion)* do eat of the crumbs falling from the table of their masters." (Matthew 15:25-27)

According to the Law, dogs were unclean animals. The term was used as a derogatory metaphor on Gentiles as to say they were morally unclean. The Greek word for "dog" was *Kuon*, such as a "wild dog." But Yahshua used a diminutive, when translated into Greek is *Kunarion*, meaning "little dog, a puppy." In texts of the Greek Scriptures, diminutives are often used to indicate affection and familiarity, such as "little sheep", or "little children." So by likening the woman to a "little dog" or puppy, and the Hebrew Israelites to "children", Yahshua was indicating who would be spiritually fed first according to his assignment.

However, notice what happened:

> "Then Yeshua answered and said unto her, O woman, great is thy faith; be it unto thee even as thou wish. And her daughter was made whole from that very hour."

Does the Gentile Times also include the prophecy of the 400 years of affliction that the Most High mentioned to Abraham in the Book of Genesis? Here it reads:

> "Then the Lord said to Abram: Know of a surety that your descendants will be foreigners in a land not theirs, and **will be slaves there, and they will be oppressed for 400 years.**" (Genesis 15:13)

Some have interpreted this passage as applying to the year 1619, when the first enslaved persons arrived in Colonial America, and ending in 2019. However, let's take a closer look. According to the above passage, the Most High was speaking to Abram (whose name He later changed to Abraham) about his descendants. According to the historical record, Abraham had many sons, his firstborn being Ishmael, and his second-born Isaac. We read at Genesis, Chapter 16 that Abraham's wife Sarah (Sarai) had been unable to conceive, and instructed her husband Abraham to have relations with Sarah's Egyptian maid servant Hagar in order to conceive a child for Sarah:

> "And Hagar bore Abram a son; and Abram called the name of his son, whom Hagar bore, Ishmael. **Abram was eighty-six years old** when Hagar bore Ishmael to Abram." (Genesis 16:15,16)

Fourteen years later, Sarah finally conceived a child named Isaac:

> "And Sarah conceived, and bore Abraham a son in his old age…**Abraham was a hundred years old** when his son Isaac was born to him." (Genesis 21:2, 5)

Before we continue this examination about the 400 year prophecy, let us ask the question: what family line did the Hebrew prophecies say the Messiah would come through? The line of Shem, **but through the Seed of Judah** (Genesis 26: 3-6; 49:9,10). **Judah was the son of Jacob, and grandson** <u>*"of Isaac*."</u>

So we continue our discussion about Abraham's descendants; On the day that Isaac was weaned, something occurred that was terribly upsetting to Sarah:

> "Now the child grew and was weaned, and Abraham prepared a big feast on the day that Isaac was weaned. But **Sarah kept noticing that the son** of Hagar the Egyptian, whom she had borne to Abraham, **was mocking Isaac.** So she said to Abraham: Drive out this slave girl and her son, for the son of this slave girl is not going to be an heir along with my son Isaac."

Sarah kept noticing that **Ishmael was mocking Isaac, making fun of Isaac in a cruel way, teasing him derisively.** Isaac at this time was only around five or six years of age, the day he had been weaned. Ishmael was about 18 or 19 years old. Fast forward, the Israelite descendants of Abraham move into Egypt and are eventually turned into slaves by Pharaoh. Soon Moses is born, runs away from Egypt, and then returns under the Most High's guidance to lead Abraham's descendants out of slavery. Notice what Moses recorded down, about that day when the Hebrew Israelites finally had left Egypt:

> "The dwelling of the Israelites, who had dwelled in Egypt and in the land of Canaan, was 430 years. At the end of the 430 years, on this very day, all the multitudes of Jehovah went out of the land of Egypt." (Exodus 12:40,41, Greek Septuagint, and Samaritan Pentateuch)

We see that, obviously, the Hebrew Israelites were not in Egypt as slaves for an entire 430 years, or even 400 years, because Moses is including part of that time to when Abraham had entered the land of Canaan, when the Most High made His covenant with Abraham. So did the prophecy of the 400 years of affliction begin with the first descendant of Abraham, and ended when Moses and the Hebrew Israelites left Egypt? If so, then when & how did the affliction begin? The 400 year affliction began when Ishmael was "mocking Isaac," **making fun of Isaac in a cruel way (this is verified at Galatians 4:29-31).** So when Moses and the Israelites departed Egypt, the 400 years of affliction mentioned at Genesis 15:13 came to an end.

However, forty years later when Moses and the Israelites were camped at the plains of Moab on the borders of Canaan, Moses explains the Law to them, and records this event in *Devarim*, where Deuteronomy 28 is explained to the Israelites what the consequences will be if they do not obey the words of the Law – *they would be put into Slavery again, "from the one end of the earth to the other end of the earth."* And that is exactly what happened again.

We are witnessing events right now in our lifetime that the ancient prophets spoke about. People are being awakened and gathered as never before, so that they can be reconnected to the promises that their ancestors had lost contact with thousands of years ago. The Trans-Atlantic Slave Trade, the Arab Slave Trade, and the events surrounding 1619 severed millions, billions, from the prophecies of the foretold Seed of Judah who was to come. Many Hebrews were led as captive slaves to the Americas, but did not know their past. Many Jews were led captive to many nations as Muslims, because they had assimilated and converted to Islam. But now we are seeing many people and language groups, some possibly "direct descendants" of the Israelite ancestors, who are processing this lost history in the Diaspora.

We are witnessing prophecy. This is the greatest opportunity for all to learn the truth about the Most High, whose name is found in the Tetragrammaton, YHWH. The ancient Hebrew Israelites wrote the divine name of the Most High with these four Hebrew consonants – YHWH, without including the vowels. But when they pronounced His name, they included the vowels.

However, today we do not know the *exact vowels* that the Hebrew Israelites used. Some say it should be pronounced "this way," some say "that way," while others say another way. Rather than debate which pronunciation should be used, what is far more important is that we are using His name that is commonly known in your particular language (For example:

Ewe – Yehowa; Igbo – Jehova; Yoruba – Jehofah; Lingala – Yawe; Luganda – Yakuwa; Samoan – Ieova; Somali – Yehowah;

Spanish – Jehova/Yahweh; Cherokee – Yihowa; Chippewa – Jehovah; Choctaw – Chihowa; Seneca – Yawen; Zulu – Jehova/Yahwe.

Very soon, Babylon the Great, including apostate Christendom, will face her fast-approaching judgment and be done away with. The word *Christendom* is not referring to only one major church denomination. It is referring to all churches who "claim" to be Christian, yet their teachings promote instead the same false pagan beliefs as were spread in the ancient city Babylon, right after that great global flood in Noah's day. As was stated in the previous chapter, the title "Babylon the Great" mentioned in the Book of Revelation is referring to false worship, "all false religion worldwide" that does not align with the original teachings of the Bible. Soon there will be no more "claims" of believing in God, while provoking ethnic and religious hatred and inciting genocides. Revelation 17:16,17 tells us what is in store for Babylon the Great:

> "And the ten horns that you saw, and the wild beast, these will hate the harlot and will make her devastated and naked, and will eat up her fleshy parts and will completely burn her with fire. For God put it into their hearts to carry out his thought...until the words of God will have been accomplished."

Before the political kings of the world turn against this blood-guilty, hypocritical worldwide religious system, what is the wisest thing we can do without delay? Notice what the Most High's servant John heard from above:

> "GET OUT OF HER, my people, if you do not want to share with her in her sins, and if you do not want to receive part of her plagues...and no light of a lamp will ever shine in you again, and **no voice of a bridegroom and of a bride will ever be heard in you again**...for by your **spiritistic** practice all the nations were misled." (Revelation 18:4, 23)

Another reason why we know the phrase "Babylon the Great" is referring to *Religion* is because notice the angel told Apostle John to write down "no voice of a bridegroom and of a bride will ever be heard in you again." Traditionally for hundreds of years, and even still today, who most often customarily officiates over the wedding of the bridegroom and the bride and where? It is usually a religious or spiritual representative of a religious entity, and most often performed in a church, shrine, synagogue, chapel, or mosque. Isn't it amazing that after thousands of years, the mystery of that phrase "Babylon the Great" has now been revealed to us.

We cannot procrastinate. If we recognize that we perhaps are still supporting any type of religious worship that does not recognize or follow the true Messiah Yeshua/Yahshua, and/or observing celebrations that come from babylonish, pagan customs, or traditions and festivals of Law under the old arrangement, then we need to "Get Out of Her" without delay.

Yeshua did not come to destroy the Law, but to fulfill it, which he did because he was perfect. However, we are not, and so the Law given at Mount Sinai remains to us as a curse and death penalty. The prophecy in Daniel said that the Messiah would "cause sacrifice and gift offering to cease." (Daniel 9:27) That is why we are now free from the Law and its holy days, new moons, and Sabbath days, and instead, follow the life pattern and teachings of our Messiah King under the new arrangement, whose shed blood is far superior than heifers. That is why the Benjamite Paul said:

> "Let no man therefore judge you in meat, or in drink, or in respect of an holyday, or of the new moon, or of the Sabbath days: Which are only a shadow of things to come; but the reality is the body of Christ." (Colossians 2:16,17)

We know that the noun "shadow" is a dark shape produced by a body coming between rays of light and a surface. The "shadow" is not the actual "body" or "object." Paul was saying that the law was only "a shadow" of things "to come." When that which is the reality "comes", do we still wish to live under the shadow? Or follow the *reality*?

Very soon an announcement will be made worldwide that this world system has achieved: "Peace and Security!" This will be announced by the Gentile nations. DO NOT BELIEVE IT. Why? Because the Most High said that when this future announcement is made – then "sudden destruction will be instantly" upon Christendom and upon all other forms of false worship, "as pangs of distress upon a pregnant woman, and they will by no means escape" (1 Thessalonians 5:3). Yeshua called this horrific event the "Great Tribulation." This world event will be sudden, unexpected. We must take action *Before* these events occur. Only the Most High can achieve *true peace and security* to this Earth, not the Gentile nations. (Matthew 24:21)

It will be just like the days of Noah. Back during that critical time period in mankind's history, there was only ONE WAY of survival – getting inside the ark that Noah and his family had built. Everyone living at that time had the opportunity to discern the expressed will and purpose of the Most High God and to follow the arrangement for survival that was open for them to be a part of. If anyone thought they were going to survive by creating their own arrangement – such as building their own boat or ship – they were gravely mistaken.

There is something else about the time of Noah that we do well to never forget – Yahuah/Yehovah proclaimed that mankind's days would come to an end during the Nephilim, *but He allowed a certain brief period of time – 120 years – before the flood waters actually came* (Genesis 6:3). Why did the Most High hold off for 120 years to destroy that generation? **Because a special work needed to be done** *before* that global flood began. The ark needed to be built and completed *before* the flood waters came down. It took Noah and his family many years before the ark was fit and ready.

The same is true today – a special work needs to be completed on earth after 1914 – *before* the king Yeshua/Yahshua takes action. What is this work?

There is only one way to survival – discerning the expressed will and purpose of the Most High, and to follow the arrangement that is being made available to us in these last days. The Benjamite Saul – he knew the Law forwards and backwards. Saul was well versed in the Hebrew Scriptures. And yet, he was hunting down and murdering the followers of Yahshua, the one who was baptized in 29 CE in the 15th year of the reign of Tiberius Caesar. Saul knew about Daniel's prophecy about the Seventy weeks. He knew about the prophecy that "the scepter would not turn away from Judah, nor the commander's staff, until Shiloh comes." He knew the prophecy at Hosea 11:1, which said *"Out of Egypt I called my son."*

Saul knew all the prophecies concerning the Coming Mashiach. He no doubt heard the reports about the miracles Hamashiach was performing, and how he was executed on Nisan 14, Passover. No doubt he heard the report that at the festival of Pentecost, *about 3,000 persons were baptized that very day* – Hebrew Jews and proselytes – when Peter stood up and explained the meaning of the events that had occurred fifty days previous. But Saul had not yet made the connection between what the scriptures said about Messiah, and what Saul was seeing and hearing. Until one day the voice of Yahshua spoke to him, and everything changed. All the knowledge of scripture that Saul had, now came to life and made complete sense of who the true Messiah was. Saul's name was changed to Paul, and he spent the rest of his earthly life tirelessly trying to help his fellow Hebrew Israelites to understand that Yahshua is the Messiah.

After his baptism, Yahshua spent the rest of his life on earth searching for the lost sheep of the house of Israel. But he also revealed there would be other persons who needed to be found:

"And I have other sheep, **which are not of this fold**, those also I must bring, and they will listen to my voice, and they will become one flock, one shepherd." (John 10:16)

These "other sheep" are not part of his "little flock" who would rule in heaven with him. Yeshua said these other sheep are not of that fold, but they would listen to his voice and become "One" flock as a united organized group. Who are these other sheep? In Revelation, after Yeshua's slave John counted the number of those who were sealed out of the Twelve Tribes of the sons of Israel, John said this:

"After these things I saw, and look! A great multitude which no man was able to number, out of all nations and tribes and peoples and tongues, standing before the throne and before the Lamb, dressed in white robes; and there were palm branches in their hands…And in response one of the elders said to me: These who are dressed in the white robes, who are they and where did they come from? So right away I said to him: "My lord, you are the one that knows." And he said to me: "These are the ones that come out of the great tribulation, and they have washed their robes and made them white in the blood of the Lamb… They will hunger no more nor thirst anymore, neither will the sun beat down upon them nor any scorching heat, because the Lamb, who is in the midst of the throne, will shepherd them and will guide them to fountains of waters of life. And God will wipe out every tear from their eyes." (Revelation 7:9,13,14,16,17)

The "other sheep" are the *Great Multitude*, who will have the hope of living here on a paradise earth. These ones do not go up to the heavenly kingdom with Yahshua and the little flock, because they are not of that fold. Rather, these "other sheep" will survive the Great Tribulation while here on earth.

True Christians, as were taught by Yahshua, are Not the enemy and never were. Our enemies are *Christendom*, who is the Man of Lawlessness, and *Babylon the Great*, the world empire of false religion, or false worship. Both enemies twisted the scriptures to try to hide the truth of the Coming Seed Yeshua, whom the Most High sent.

Christendom's historical apostate record has stumbled many away from the truth revealed by Yeshua/Yahshua. But as was already discussed, Christendom and all of Babylon the Great, along with the wild beast, which represent the political system of this world, will be done away with forever. No more religious wars, terrorism, and genocide, such as we see now with the Anglo-American world power, the seventh head of the wild beast.

The Most High does not hate or block anyone *who is seeking to know Him* in humility and truth. The Most High Yahuah/Yehovah welcomes anyone who wishes, to follow Him by means of the new arrangement He has put in place through His son, the foretold anointed Seed. The Most High has appointed Yeshua/Yahshua the King [his name when translated to Spanish is "Jesus," but not Christendom's Jesus], to gather all the dispersed ones to now share in the final assignment that Yahshua has given:

"And this good news of the Kingdom will be preached **as a witness** to all the nations, and then the end will come." (Matthew 24:14)

Then Yahshua's Kingdom will reign without any rivals. *Soon a paradise earth will be reality*. No more hatred. No more Racism. No more pain. No more sickness. No more war. No more greedy nations fighting over control of the natural resources of the earth, such as we see today in the Congo and other countries.

<u>**Does a person have to move to Africa or to a particular area in Africa to be saved**</u>? **No.** The prophets Ezekiel and Isaiah prophesied that no matter where one lives, you may come under the Most High's protection from Gog of Magog if one is a part of His new arrangement:

> "Son of man, set your face against **Gog of the land of Magog**…And it must occur in that day that things will come up into your heart, and **you will certainly think up an injurious scheme, and you will say: I shall go up against the land of open rural country**, I shall come in upon those having no disturbance, dwelling in security, all of them dwelling without wall, and they do not have even bar and doors… *Come, my people, enter thou into thy chambers, and shut thy doors about thee: hide thyself as it were for a little moment, until the indignation be over-past."* (Ezekiel 38:2, 10-12; Isaiah 26:20)

We notice the prophet said that Gog of Magog will go up against the land of open rural country. This is not speaking of any literal country or continent. The prophet is speaking about the *"symbolic" country of Spiritual Protection and Security of His people, no matter where one lives!* Notice the prophet says to "enter into thy chambers." *The "chambers" are meeting-places around the globe where the Most High's people congregate to receive life-giving instructions within His new arrangement of true worship, which is no longer in Babylon the Great.*

> "And they gathered them together to **the place** that is called in Hebrew Har-Magedon [Mountain of Megiddo/Assembly of Troops]." (Revelation 16:16)

The Greek word for "place" is *topon*, which means, not a physical geographic location, but means *"a condition or situation."*

Notice also this: The welcoming of our dead loved ones will take place here on earth in the Resurrection. Note what the Most High says:

> **"If a man dies, can he live again? All the days of my appointed time will I wait, till my change comes. Thou shalt call, and I will answer thee...***And he will wipe out every tear from their eyes, and death will be no more, neither will mourning nor outcry nor pain be anymore. The former things have passed away.*** (Job 14:14, 15; Revelation 21:4)

Just imagine when that takes place in a paradise earth: Welcoming our loved ones back, perhaps a parent, grandparents, great-grandparents, great-great-grandparents, great-great-great-great-great-great-grandparents, perhaps those who lived & died in the South on the plantations, who were buried after dying in the cotton fields, or those ancestors who watched their families split apart and sold away on the auction blocks. They too, will be reunited with their loved ones again, even reunited with the ancestors whom they were taken away from in the motherland. Yahuah/Yehovah and Yeshua/Yahshua will make it happen.

The Gentile Times have ended! All The nations are now on borrowed time, because Yeshua/Yahshua/Jesus/Hesus is now preparing for battle.

Barnett, Lipscomb, & Land of the Hebrews

So, what about FPOC Charles Barnett of Albemarle County, Virginia – Did I finally learn that he was indeed an ancestor to my paternal Grandmother Marcella Barnett? And, did I ever discover the truth behind the statement my mother's grandfather said – Julius Lipscomb Jr. – that he was a "Black Jew?"

Charles Barnett of Albemarle County, Virginia actually did live to be 100 years old, as shown on the 1850 Virginia census, and living next door to several Goins families. I also discovered that Charles had children. Inside his pension file was a letter dated July 31, 1849, stating that Charles Barnett had children in Granville County, North Carolina. However, I was unable to find the names of his children, and therefore, could not prove a connection to my paternal great-great-grandfather Benjamin Barnett, who stated he was **born in Virginia** around 1835. I did find the obituary to Benjamin Barnett's wife, Jane. The only thing I was able to glean from it was that Jane Barnett said she was **born in Virginia** on May 11, 1830.

Now to my mother's ancestors – were they Hebrew Jews? The furthest I could go back on my mother's ancestors were her 2nd great-grandparents, Kit and Leah, who had both been born sometime around 1810, and living on Dabney Lipscomb's plantation in

Columbus, Mississippi, where he moved to after leaving Tuscaloosa County, Alabama in the 1830's. My mother's great-grandfather, Julius Lipscomb Sr. (Kit's son) had reported he was born in Alabama, so that made sense. According to the census, Kit, a carpenter, stated he was born in South Carolina. Leah stated she was born in Georgia (both States held the Gullah people). Oddly, that was similar to both birthplaces of plantation owner Dabney Lipscomb, born in South Carolina (in 1803), and his wife, Jane Hardwick Lipscomb, from Georgia. I surmised from this that Kit's wife Leah probably came to the plantation as a result of Dabney Lipscomb's marriage to Jane Hardwick, since it was customary in the South in slavery times for a bride (Jane Hardwick) to be given one or more "slaves" as part of her dowry, a wedding gift from her parents.

Dabney Lipscomb would have been only five years old when Kit was born. So whose land property would Kit have been living on when he and Dabney were both growing up? It would have been on the land of Dabney's parents, Joel Lipscomb and Betsey Elizabeth Chiles, in Abbeville, South Carolina. I surmised this was where Kit was probably born at, around 1808, and where Kit's parents lived. Who were Kit's parents?

In 1822, Dabney Lipscomb's parents later moved to Erie, Alabama. His father Joel Lipscomb died in 1836. An estate inventory list of thirty-two enslaved was produced. Dabney Lipscomb's mother Betsey Elizabeth received 7 slaves as her dower on December 29, 1836. **One of the slaves was the woman named Omey, sometimes spelled Omay. <u>This name is an Igbo word:</u>**

Omalicha, which means "Beautiful girl/lady"
Omasilachi, a female name
Omelora, which means "Giving, or helping people"

Ome, which means "Shoot/stem of a plant"

Omee, which means "A doer; Someone who does something"

I was unable to identify if Kit was related to Omey, but I feel that he was. Omey was on the Lipscomb plantation the same time as Kit's parents. The woman Omey had two children, <u>Clarisa and Boston</u>, who were sold away on January 18, 1848 to Dabney Lipscomb's brother Nathan Lipscomb, of Marengo County, Alabama. Grandmother Lucy had told me (in 1990) that her grandmother's name was "Leah **Dotson**." Is it possible that her name was actually Leah **Boston**? At any rate, I was amazed that Grandmother Lucy still recalled Leah's last name. That name had traveled through time.

One of the ethnic groups in Nigeria are the Igbo, who are documented to at least the 1400's in the ancient Benin Kingdom of West Africa. Among them are Igbo Jews, who say they are descendants of the Tribe of Gad through Eri, son of Gad, one of the twelve sons of Yacob (Jacob).

Was the name "Kit" an Ethiopian name? The name Kit comes from the Greek name "Kristopher." It was also a Amharic name for males in Ethiopia/Abysinnia: "Krestos" (Kristos) and "Krestosawi" (Kristosawi), which means "Bearer of the Christ."

The only other thing I can say is that my Dna test shows 9 percent "Benin/Togo" (from Bight of Benin, Juda region), 25 percent "Congo" (Land of the Jews, Abysinnia/Kongo region), and 35 percent "Nigerian" (Benin Kingdom, Bight of Biafra).

This journey has opened my eyes to many things. How Slavery started in Colonial America, *how it really started*. The event of 1619 is mainly viewed from a historical lens. However, they should also be viewed through a redemptive one, the lens of restorative justice. *Heirs rights!* True, the vestiges of Slavery still exist worldwide. But there is true hope – one day Slavery in all its forms will be gone forever. How do we know this?

Because the Most High told the ancient prophets to write it all down, to stop everything you are doing, and watch for the Sign, so not to miss it.

Comments, Chat, or Questions, email the author at: shankbibletalk@yahoo.com

Please also check out the author's favorite website: jw.org

Sources

Chapter 1
Mbundu or Ambundu people, Wikipedia
Kongo people, Ibid
Kingdom of Ndongo, Ibid

Chapter 2
1880 Federal Census, Claiborne County, MS
1900 Federal Census, Claiborne County, MS
1910 Federal Census, Claiborne, County, MS

Missouri State Board of Health, Bureau of Vital Statistics
Louise Knox, Certificate of Death

Mississippi Department of Archives and History
Dabney Lipscomb, Lowndes County, Inventories, 1850

Greene County Alabama Courthouse
Joel Lipscomb, Inventory, 1836

Chapter 3
Exodus, Issues Involved. (Israelites and Egyptians intermarried) *Insight On The Scriptures*, Volume 1, pg 780, paragraph 4. Watchtower Bible And Tract Society of New York, Inc. International Bible Students Association, 1988. Brooklyn, New York

Phinehas: *The Oxford companion to the Bible*, pg 10-11. Oxford University Press, New York, 1993

#6372, "Pe-nehasi, the Negro." *Brown-Driver-Briggs. A Hebrew and English Lexicon of the Old Testament.* England, 1906

The Egyptian Origin of Some English Personal Names, pg 192. Journal of the American Oriental Society, Jun., 1936, Vol. 56, No. 2

The Evidence for the Authenticity of the Wilderness Tradition, pg 226. James K. Hoffmeier

Phineas. Ancestry.com

Panehesy (name). Wikipedia
Panehsy (TT16). ibid

The Manners and Customs of the Ancient Egyptians. Wilkinson, John Gardner. Vol.1, Pg 2. "The name of Ham is, in fact, the same as that of Egypt, Khem, or Cham"

Assyria, *Insight On The Scriptures*, Volume 1, pg 201..Watchtower Bible And Tract Society of New York, Inc. International Bible Students Association, 1988. Brooklyn, New York

Eber, pg 673, ibid

Ewe people, Wikipedia

Hebrew Eve (1): Who are the Eve people? YouTube video. By Hebrew Ivri Ewe Eve The Black Man. L. Seyram Adzanku

How Togo came to have its name. African Lisbon Tour, April 19, 2020. africanlisbontour.com

Amarna letters, Wikipedia

The Merneptah Stele. Egyptian Museum, Cairo

Eliezer Ben Hurcanus. Wikipedia

Pirkei DeRabbi Eliezer, Chapter 24. https://www.sefaria.org

Gregory vs. Baugh, 1827. Caseload Access Project, htps://case.law
Pope vs. Anderson, 1858. Ibid

Samuel Stanhope Smith, in *Freud, Race, and Gender*. Gilman, Sander L. Princeton, 1993. Pg 375

Origin of Mankind, Africa/Europe. *The Destruction of Black Civilization*. Williams, Chancellor. Chicago. Pg 42

Chapter 4

Second Kansas Colored Volunteer Infantry Regiment (1863-1865). Blackpast.org

Arkansas Civil War Battles, National Park Service www.nps.gov;

Skirmish at Saline Bottom. Encyclopedia of Arkansas. https://encyclopediaofarkansas.net;

Saline Bottoms. camdenexpedition.org

1870 Federal Census, Douglas County, KS
1880 Federal Census, Wyandotte County, KS

Abstracts of Douglas County Petitions for Divorce (1864-1884)
The Pioneer, Douglas County Genealogical Society, Vol VIII, No 2

www.centralvirginiahistory.org
Free People of Color: 18th Century Residents
By Robert Vernon

www.findagrave.com
Edwin Hickman (1690 – 1769) Albemarle County, Virginia
Source: Ron Stephens
Library of Virginia

Albemarle County Order Book, 1795-1798, pg 137
Albemarle County Will Book, 5:77
Albemarle County Marriage Book 1, 1786-1805, pg 19

Revolutionary War Pensions
Charles Barnett, Certificate of Freedom
Charles Barnett, bondsman

http://revwarapps.org
Southern Campaign American Revolution Pension Statements
Charles Barnett, S8048
Transcribed and annotated by C. Leon Harris

www.freeafricanamericans.com
List of Free African Americans in the Revolution
by Paul Heinegg

The Archaeology of Bowles' Lot:
Phase III Data Recovery Excavations at 44AB374,
A Late 18th – 19th Century Free African-American Rural Domestic Site in
    Albemarle County, Virginia
Stephen M. Thompson, Principal Investigator, Report Author
Rivanna Archaeological Services, Charlottesville, VA (January 2010)

Chapter 5
*Akee Tree, A Descendant's Quest For His Slave Ancestors on the Eskridge
    Plantations.*
By Stephen Hanks (2013)

Family Records, private collection, Jack Grantham Jr.

www.magnoliasandpeaches.com
Grantham Family, by Scott Owens

www.findagrave.com
Susannah Grantham Guice (1789-1863) Jefferson County, MS
Source: Anthony Miller

1860 Federal Census, Wayne County, NC
1870 Federal Census, Wayne County, NC

Chapter 6
1850 Federal Census, Ozark County, MO
1870 Federal Census, Texas County, MO
1880 Federal Census, Douglas County, MO
1900 Federal Census, Howell County, MO

A History of Ozark County 1841-1991
Ozarks County Genealogical and Historical Society (1991)

"One More Mountain to Cross"
By Frankie Blackburn, with Brenda Collins Dillon, Joyce Lea Kollenberg,
    Cynthia Jane Steeley,
John Trulinger
Appalachian Quarterly, Wise County Historical Society, Wise County, VA
    (1998)

Hall Family:
Howell County Gazette, June 16, 1910
1850 Federal Census, Oregon County, MO
1860 Federal Census, Howell County, MO
Files.usgwarchives.net – Maury County Tennessee / Court
Submitter: William Allen Holmes

Library of Virginia
Louisa County Order Books, 1742-1748

Chapter 7
www.blackpast.org
Jessie Dwight Locker

1850 Federal Census Slave Schedules, Panola County, TX
1860 Federal Census Slave Schedules, Hunt County, TX
1870 Federal Census, Hunt County, TX
1880, 1900, 1910 Federal Census, Rains County, TX
Rains County Leader, December 2, 1921
Henry Ivey, obituary

Claude News, January 9, 1931
Henry Ivey, "Richest Citizen of County Was a Negro"

http://sos.tn.gov
Tennessee State Archives, Supreme Court Cases
Court case: Jack vs. Foust, (1877)
Kingsport Times, August 3, 1923 pg 12 – Judge Lewis Shepherd

1812 Court Trial, Thomas Hagans
North Carolina Genealogy Society Journal, Vol IX, pg 259

North Carolina State Archives
Colonial Land Entries in North Carolina 1769-1774, by A.B. Pruitt
General Assembly Records, December 1773, Box 6
Tax Lists of Bladen County, Vol II, pg 143
Richmond County, NC Land Entries 1780-1795, by A.B. Pruitt

South Carolina Historical Society
Marlboro County Will Book A – James Ivey, 1820

Chapter 8
www.eclectica.org
MALUNGU: The African Origin of the American Melungeons
By Tim Hashaw (2001)

www.lva.virginia.gov – Tithables
Government And Labor In Early America, IX
By Richard B. Morris (1946)

Virginia Council and General Court Records, 1640-1641,
The Virginia Magazine of History and Biography, Vol. 11, No 3 (January
    1904)
Published by Virginia Historical Society

York County Deeds, Orders, and Wills (3) 16, 26 January 1657/8
Library of Virginia, Colonial Papers, folder 19, no. 2, Record Group 1

www.freeafricanamericans.com
Gowen / Going Family – Thomas Gowen (Michael) born say 1660

Chapter 9

www.encyclopediavirginia.org
Virginia's First Africans
By Martha McCartney

New Light on the '20 and Odd Negroes' Arriving in Virginia
By Engel Sluiter
William and Mary Quarterly, 3d ser., 54 (1997)

*A Study of the Africans and African Americans on Jamestown Island and at
    Green Spring, 1619-1803*
By Martha W. McCartney (National Park Service and Colonial
    Williamsburg Foundation, 2003)

The Devil's Lane: Sex and Race in the Early South
By Catherine Clinton, Michele Gillespie (1997)

http://memory.loc.gov
The Library of Congress > American Women
Slavery and Indentured Servants (Virginia Laws, Act XII)

The Statutes at Large, Laws of Virginia
By William Waller Hening (1823)

Proceedings of the Virginia Assembly, 1619, in *Narratives of Early Virginia, 1606-1625*
By Lyon Gardiner Tyler (1959)

www.history.org/history/teaching/slavelaw
Slavery and the Law in Virginia

Colored Freemen As Slave Owners In Virginia
The Journal of Negro History, Vol. I, June 1916, No. 3, pgs 233-237

Headright, Wikipedia
John Punch, ibid
John Casor, ibid
Anthony Johnson (colonist), ibid

Virginia Council and General Court Records, 1640-1641,
The Virginia Magazine of History and Biography, Vol 11, No 3 (January 1904)
Published by Virginia Historical Society

Chapter 10

New York City's Slave Market, by Sylviane Diouf, New York Public Library (2015)

Newnetherlandinstitute.org/Slavery in New Netherland

The Freedmen of New Amsterdam, by Peter R. Christoph, Selected Rensselaerswijck Seminar Papers, A Beautiful And Fruitful Place, Volume 1 (1991) New York State Library

Slave Market, Mapping the African American Past, https://maap.columbia.edu

The Project Gutenberg eBook, Journal of Jasper Danckaerts, 1679 – 1680, by Jasper Danckaerts, Edited by Barlett Burleigh James and J. Franklin Jameson, Translated by Henry C. Murphy

Slavery in New York, by New York Historical Society

The Atlantic Slave Trade Continued Illegally in America Until the Civil War, History Stories, by John Harris, Jan 28, 2021

Wanderer (Slave ship) Wikipedia

Chapter 11

www.blackpast.org
Anthony Johnson, John Johnson Jr.

www.geni.com
Josiah Collins, II (1778 – 1831)

Melungeons, A Multi-Ethnic Population
By Roberta J. Estes, Jack H. Goins, Penny Ferguson, Janet Lewis Crain (2012)
Melungeon DNA Project

Free African Americans of North Carolina and Virginia
by Paul Heinegg (1997)
Third Edition

The SAGE Encyclopedia of African Cultural Heritage in North America
Edited by Mwalimu J. Shujaa, Kenya J. Shujaa (2015)

Slavery and Identity: Ethnicity, Gender, and Race in Salvador, Brazil, 1808-1888
By Mieko Nishida (2003)

The Comparative Histories of Slavery in Brazil, Cuba, and the United States
By Laird W. Bergad (2007)

MALUNGU: The African Origin of the American Melungeons,
Part 1, The Kimbundu-Angolan Origin Of The Name "Melungeon"
By Tim Hashaw (2001)

www.nytimes.com
Obama's Mother Had African Forebear, Study Suggests
(July 30, 2012)

www.wargs.com
Ancestry of Barack Obama
Compiled by William Addams Reitwiesner
Ann Dunham, Wikipedia

Elizabeth Key Grinstead, ibid
Stono Rebellion, ibid

Johnny Depp
USA Today – "Lone Ranger' stars have roots in historic figures
(June 26, 2013)

Chris Tucker
www.npr.org National Public Radio
Documentary Traces Roots of Black Celebrities
(February 14, 2006)

http://bigthink.com
Why Were The Melungeons Surprised By Their African Roots?
By Kris Broughton (May 26, 2012)

History of Crete, Wikipedia

Bulletin de la Societe Languedocienne de Geographie. Montpellier, 1890.
Vol. 13, pg 272

The Earth And Its Inhabitants. Reclus, Elisee. Princeton, 1888. Pg 267

Jews in Jamaica and Suriname. *The Lost Tribes A Myth.* Allen H. Godbey. Pg
252

North African Jewish and non-Jewish populations form distinctive, orthogonal clusters. Published in the Proceedings of the National Academy of Sciences, August 6, 2012. DNA analysis shows North African Jews originated in biblical-era Israel.

The History of African Gene Flow into Southern Europeans, Levantines, and Jews. PLOS, Genetics, April 2011

Chapter 12

1. *Annals.* Tacitus. Book 1

2. Augustus. Wikipedia

3. The *Lives of the Caesars.* Suetonius

4. *Fasti Antiates Ministrorum Domas Augustae* (Ancient Roman Calendar of Officially Commemorated Events). Appendix II. Pg 141 (Pg 146 digital version). "Augustus 17th September Deification" (AD 14)

5. *Ezra and Nehemiah: Their Lives and Times.* Rawlinson, George. London, 1890. Pgs 21,22

Chapter 13

1.*Antiquities of the Jews.* Josephus. Book 20, Chapter 9

2. *Annals.* Tacitus. Book 15, Paragraph 44

3. Gemara, Sanhedrin 43a. *Babylonian Talmud, Munich Codex* (Hebrew Manuscript 95)
"Yeshu *the Nazarean* was hanged on the eve of *Passover.*"
(In other editions, Rabbi Dr. H. Freedman makes a footnote "Nazarean" from Munich Codex)

4. *Dialogue with Trypho.* Justin Martyr. Chapter 108, #235. Apparently on the third day the body was not found in the tomb.

5. Quotes from *The Acts of Pontius Pilate* contained in *First Apology of Justin Martyr*. Chapters 35 and 48

Chapter 14

The Expulsion of 612 CE. *The Lost Tribes A Myth*. Allen H. Godbey. Pg 218.

Spain, Visigoths And The Jews. The Incredible Story Of The Jewish People. JewishWikipedia.Info

The Jews in Spain Under the Visigoths, by Dr. Julian Furst. The Occident And American Jewish Advocate. Vol. VII, No. 8. Marcheshvan 5610, November 1849

Life of Constantine. Eusebius. Vol. III, Chapter XVIII

Constantine. *Ecclesiastical History*. Theodoret. Book 1, Chapter 9

The Cross a Pagan Symbol. *The Two Babylons*. Hislop. Pg 201.

The Jews In Europe. *History Of The Jews*. Graetz. Chapter II

Periplus of Hanno. Codex Palatines Graecus 398. University of Heidelberg library. World Encyclopedia.

The Periplus of Hanno/Chapter 2. *THE GEOGRAPHY OF THE VOYAGE OF HANNO*. Wikisource.org

Senegal River (mistaken by the Portuguese for the Nile) *History of India*. Jackson, A.V. Williams. London, 1906. Pg 59

Chapter 15

The Jews of Africa. Sidney Mendelsson, pgs 2, 5,6, 9-11, 16-20. 1920, New York

"The Land of the Hebrews." *A Geographical History of Africa*. Leo Africanus, translated by John Pory

Falashas – Beta Israel, Jewish Encyclopedia, by J.D. Perruchon, Richard Gottheil

Emperor Susenyos, Dailykos.com

Travels to Discover the Source of the Nile, Volume 3, pgs 308, 435-437. James Bruce

Slavery in Ethiopia, Wikipedia

Kingdom of Kaffa, Wikipedia

Ethiopian Emperors and Slavery, Hanibal Goitom. Library of Congress

How Portuguese Slave Traders Changed Ethiopia and Congo, by Livia Gershon, October 5, 2023, JSTOR Daily

Shanqella, Wikipedia

Shanqella, global.museum-digital.org

Africans in Colonial Louisiana. Gwendolyn Midlo Hall. Louisiana State University Press, 1995.

Joseph de Villar Dubreuil, Dictionary of Louisiana Biography – D, Louisiana Historical Association. Lahistory.org>resources

Mapping Uncertainty, The Collapse of Oyo and the Trans-Atlantic Slave Trade, 1816-1836, by Henry B. Lovejoy, in Journal of Global Slavery, Volume 4 Issue 2 (2019)

Slaves from The Bight of Benin Vs The Bight of Biafra – Numbers & Cultural Legacy – Culture – Nigeria by bigfrancis21, January 19, 2017. Nairaland Forum

The Encyclopedia of Caribbean Religions, pgs 72-746; pgs 1134-1139. Patrick Taylor and Frederick Case. 2013

Netzach Yisrael, Chapter 34, by Sage Yehuda Loewe. 1599. Sefaria.org

Jerusalem Talmud Sanhedrin, Chapter 10. *Where are the Ten Lost Tribes of Israel?* By Yehuda Shurpin. Chabad.org

Midrash Pesikta Rabbati, Chapter 31. *Where are the Ten Lost Tribes of Israel?* By Yehuda Shurpin. Chabad.org

Virginia Slave-Trade Statistics 1698 – 1775, pgs 47-65. Walter Minchinton, Celia King, Peter Waite. Virginia State Library, Richmond, 1984

'Unable to distinguish between a Jew from a Mohammedan.' *The Lost Tribes A Myth.* Godbey. Pg 219. Internet Archives

Ibid, Pg 267 (digital page). The Fulani's belief they are descendants of Ham's son Put, or Phut.

Ibid, Pg 246. "Judaized Negroes were among the slaves brought to America."

America, Being The Latest And Most Accurate Description of the New World. By Arnoldus Montanus; John Ogilby. 1671. Pg 574. Jews sold as slaves to Sao Tome.

The Interesting Narrative of the Life of Olaudah Equiano, Or, Gustavus Vassa, The African. Equiano, Olaudah. London. 1789

Slave Life in Georgia: A Narrative of the Life, Sufferings, and Escape of John Brown, a Fugitive Slave, Now in England. By John Brown, Edited by L.A. Chamerovzow, Secretary of the British and Foreign Anti-Slavery Society. London, 1855. Electronic version 2001; Documenting the American South https://docsouth.unc.edu

Autobiography of Omar Ibn Said, Slave in North Carolina, 1831. The American Historical Review, 30, No. 4 (July 1925), Pgs 787-795, John Franklin Jameson, ed.

Enslaved And Freed African Muslims. Muslim Slaves in America. Lowcountry Digital History Initiative. Ldhi.library.cofc.edu

The Gospels Written in the Negro Patois of English, with Arabic Characters, By a Mandingo Slave, by William B. Hodgson

Affairs of West Africa. Morel. Chapter XVI, "The Fulani in West African History." Pgs 130-150.

Judeo-Arabic dialects. Wikipedia

Ibid, Judaeo-Spanish

Ibid, Andalusi Arabic/Andalusi Romance

A Description of Timbuktu. Africanus, Leo. 1526

Map of the Congo. 1619 – Twenty Africans. Stephen Hanks. 2019. Pg 94

Sweetgrass Baskets And The Gullah Tradition. Coakley, Joyce V. Charleston, 2005

Inside a controversial auction of Gullah-Geechee homes: This land needs to be protected, by Justin Glawe, Cotton Capital: ongoing series. South Carolina, The Guardian, Nov. 3, 2019

Chapter 16

Book of Ezra. *Encyclopedia Americana*. 1953. Vol 10 Pg 689. **The Jews returned to Jerusalem in 537 BCE**

"COMING" *Parousia. An Expository Dictionary of New Testament Words*. Vine, W.E. London, 1940. Pg 208, 209

John Wycliff. Wikipedia

Ibid, William Tyndale

Ibid, Michael Servetus

Those About To Die. Mannix, David. New York, 1958. Pg 135, 137. The Original Christians

The New World's Foundation in the Old. Ruth West and Willis Mason West. Boston, 1929. Pg 131

Early Christians in Roman Empire. H. Ingli James, quoted in *Treasury of the Christian World*. Gordon Nasby, ed. New York, 1953. Pg 369

The Birth of a Nation, Wikipedia

Watch Tower Bible & Tract Society of New York. International Bible Students Association. *Thy Kingdom Come*. 1891. Pg 305

Ibid, *The Time is at Hand*. 1889. Pg 170

Ibid, *Jehovah's Witnesses, Proclaimers of God's Kingdom*. 1993. Pg 134, 135, 719, 720

"Admonish," *Chrematizo*, pg 31. "Called", pg 163. W.E. Vine's *Expository Dictionary of New Testament Words*

CROSS. *Parousia. An Expository Dictionary of New Testament Words*. Vine, W.E. London, 1940. Vol. 1, Pg 256

Christmas. The Catholic Encyclopedia, 1908, Vol. III, Pg 724

Dies Natalis Solis Invicti (Roman festival on December 25)

Date of Birth of Jesus. Wikipedia

The World Book Encyclopedia, 196, Vol. 3, Pg 416

Encyclopedia of Religion and Ethics, by James Hastings, Vol III, Pg 608,609

Birthdays. The Catholic Encyclopedia, New York, 1911. Vol. X, Pg 709

Exhaustive Concordance Of The Bible. Strong, James. Madison, NJ, 1890

Some of the Kings of the North and of the South in Daniel Chapter 11:

North	South
Syrian King Seleucus I Nicator	The Ptolemy Dynasty
The German Empire	Britain
Nazi Hitler's Third Reich	Anglo-American World Power
USSR Communist bloc	Anglo-American World Power
Russia	Anglo-American World Power

Chapter 17

Esau's wives: Genesis 36:2, 3

Edomites and Judaism: *Jewish Antiquities*, by Josephus. XIII, 257,258; XV, 253, 254

Chapter 18

"They will Be Led Captive" Aichmalotos, #164. *Exhaustive Concordance Of The Bible*. Strong, James. Madison, NJ, 1890

Luke 21:24, pg 293. *The Emphatic Diaglott Containing The Original Greek Text*, By Benjamin Wilson. Originally published 1864.

An Expository Dictionary of New Testament Words. Vine, W.E. London, 1940. "DOG" *Kunarion* Pg 332

An Expository Dictionary of New Testament Words. Vine, W.E. London, 1940. "PLACE" *Topos*. Vol III, Pg 185

Requested Photo Credits

All Photos from Wikimedia Commons unless noted otherwise.

1. African Slave Traders Traveling to a Slave Market

2. Burning of a Village in Africa and Capture of its Inhabitants

3. African Slaves transport

4. The Capture of Slaves

5. Slaves Waiting for Sale – Richmond

6. Slave Hunt, Dismal Swamp, by Thomas Moran

7. Drummer at Hamed

8. Ethiopian Women at Kotel

9. Arab Women in Jerusalem carrying containers filled with Labaneh

10. 12 Tribes of Israel

11. Map of Togoland, 1914, the Slave Coast

12. Map of the Oyo Empire, Bight of Benin, by Henry B. Lovejoy

13. Portrait of Pope Nicholas V, by Peter Paul Rubens

14. Whore of Babylon, from Martin Luther's 1534 translation of the Bible (This file has been identified as being free of known restriction under copyright law, including all related and neighboring rights)

15. African Slave Ship Cargo.

16. First Slave Auction, 1655, New Amsterdam (New York)

17. Land of the Jews, 1588, by Livio Sanuto

18. Bambara Territory, West Africa,1819, by Thomas Bowdich

19. North Carolina Newspaper Article in 1853, Negro Jews (Public Domain)

20. North Carolina Newspaper Article, the Bambara (Public Domain)

21. Woman-Slave, Enslaved girl – New Orleans 1850

22. Bambara Girl

23. Wilson Chinn a Branded Slave from Louisiana

24. Battlefield of Gettysburg

25. International Bible Students (Author's Collection)

26. The Flight of the Prisoners, by James Tissot (Public Domain)

27. Britain Declares War, 1914 (Public Domain)

28. Sweet Potato Planting, Hopkinson's Plantation 1862

29. Negro Slaves 1862, Edisto Island, SC

30. Black Cotton-Farming Family (1890's)

31. Emancipated Slaves Brought from Louisiana

32. BOOK COVER PHOTO – Israelite Slaves In Egypt Making Bricks (Public Domain)

www.ingramcontent.com/pod-product-compliance
Lightning Source LLC
Chambersburg PA
CBHW051244020426
42333CB00025B/3037